*The Quest for the*

# AMERICA'S CUP

*Sailing to Victory*

## Richard V. Simpson

Charleston · London

THE
History
PRESS

Published by The History Press
Charleston, SC 29403
www.historypress.net

*Front cover*: Captain Nat's swift cup defenders, the *Constitution* (foreground) and the *Columbia*.
*Back Cover*: Nat Herreshoff's Noble Trio: the *Reliance* (left), the *Columbia* (center) and the *Constitution*.

First published 2012

Manufactured in the United States

ISBN 978.1.60949.634.0

Library of Congress Cataloging-in-Publication Data

Simpson, Richard V.
The quest for America's Cup : sailing to victory / Richard V. Simpson.
p. cm.
Includes bibliographical references.
ISBN 978-1-60949-634-0
1. America's Cup--History. 2. Yacht racing--History. 3. Yachts--Design and construction--
History. I. Title.
GV829.S563 2012
797.1'4--dc23
2012008226

*Notice*: The information in this book is true and complete to the best of our knowledge. It is offered without guarantee on the part of the author or The History Press. The author and The History Press disclaim all liability in connection with the use of this book.

# CONTENTS

Preface                                                              5
Acknowledgements                                                     7
The America's Cup                                                    9
Introduction                                                        11

1. The Yacht *America*                                              13
2. Blue Ribbon Sailors                                             16
3. The Racing Machines                                             23
4. The 1893 and 1895 Matches                                       26
5. Biographical Sketches of Principal Players                      32
6. The Lipton Campaigns                                            45
7. New Rules, New Challengers                                      65
8. The J-Boats Are a' Coming                                       71
9. Secrets and Spies                                               83
10. Beam, Keel, Weight and Tactics                                85
11. Still Shipshape 'n' Bristol Fash'n                             90
12. The 1980 Challenge: A Challenger and Defender Overview         97
13. 1983 Australia's Cup                                          102
14. The 1992 Match: *America³* v. *Il Moro di Venezia*            105
15. The 1995 Match: *Black Magic* v. *Young America*              112
16. The 2010 Match: *Alinghi5* v. *BMW Oracle*                    115

Appendix: Historical Chronology                                   117
Notes                                                             121
Bibliography                                                      123

# CONTENTS

Index                                    125
About the Author                         127

# PREFACE

The principle storyline in my 2010 title, *America's Cup: Trials & Triumphs*, is a nuts-and-bolts narrative about large oceangoing, wind-driven yachts; you might say it is an owner's manual for the armchair sailor.

In this book, we explore some challenges and defenses mounted by wealthy yachtsmen, captains of industry who expended huge sums of money to capture the celebrated Cup. Certainly, each challenger and defender harbors his personal reason for the chase. I believe at the root, it is for the intrinsic value of the Cup and for the prestige earned by the yacht's owner and skipper, either professional or amateur, who captures it.

The design and construction of a large sail yacht is a complicated matter. During the course of years between challenges and defenses, designs, building materials and the shape of yachts have altered dramatically. Advancements in marine architecture and hardware have greatly changed the character of oceanracing yachts over the past 150 years; consider the change from wood to metal and to today's carbon fiber technology.

Until the mid-twentieth century, the America's Cup yacht race was largely a private affair, a sport enjoyed by the privileged few. Today, with the advent of 'round-the-clock electronic satellite coverage, it is a major international sporting event viewed by many millions, ranking only slightly below the Olympic Games.

For this narrative, I have searched dozens of century-old magazines, gazettes and tabloids for examples of these advancements. In addition, it is interesting to read the comments of insiders—owners, designers and builders—and the observations of contemporary sportswriters whose words appeared in prestigious period magazines and newspapers no longer in publication. The text, photographs and illustrations for *The Quest for America's Cup* are from diverse sources, and every effort was made to identify those sources.

Illustrations are from nineteenth-century stereo view photos and periodicals, newspaper wire photos and period postcards. Generally, text is from mid- to late nineteenth-century newspapers and commercial books, sports magazines and yacht syndicate promotional pamphlets.

# ACKNOWLEDGEMENTS

S incere thanks to Kristan McClintock, Hall Spars' director of marketing, and Eric Hall for supplying the in-depth history of the genesis and successes of Hall Spars.

This iconic image of Captain Nat appeared in the September 1901 issue of *Harper's New Monthly Magazine*. The photo's caption says Captain Nat is watching a race between the *Shamrock* and the *Columbia* from the New York Yacht Club committee boat.

# THE AMERICA'S CUP

The celebrated Cup originally referred to as the "Royal Yacht Squadron Cup" or the "RYS Cup for 100 Sovereigns" subsequently became known as the America's Cup after the name of the boat that first won it. The Cup, created in 1848, is the work of R&S Gerrard Ltd., Silversmiths, England.

Gerrard's description of the trophy reads:

> *The America's Cup, silver, in the form of a ewer, round spread foot, the stem decorated with a bead band and geometric strapwork, the lower body chased with pellet and further architectural strapwork enclosing burnished panels, the upper body lobe fluted, each lobe engraved with an inscription and separated by masks and strapwork, the baluster neck stippled and chased with foliate scrolls and anthemion motifs above a band of pellets centre with flower heads on a background of horizontal lines, similarly chased rim to the spout, bead decorated flying scroll and baluster handle.*

From *Leslie's Weekly Illustrated* newspaper, dated September 21, 1901, we learn: "The Cup is now kept in Tiffany's safe-deposit vault and shown at intervals to only a favored few, or brought out perhaps at a [New York Yacht] club dinner."

In March 1997, a person entered the Royal New Zealand Yacht Squadron's clubroom and damaged the America's Cup with a sledgehammer. The attacker, a recidivist petty criminal, claimed the attack was politically motivated; a court convicted him of malicious damage to private property and sentenced him to prison. The damage was so severe that it was feared that the Cup was irreparable. London's Gerrard Silversmiths, which had manufactured the Cup in 1848, painstakingly restored the trophy to its original condition over three months, free of charge. In 2003, an extra twenty centimeters was added to the Cup's base to accommodate the names of future winners.

# INTRODUCTION

S ailing for the singular enjoyment of the act of sailing is one of America's oldest forms of recreation. Our colonial period forebears pursued the sport, although from their sober view of life they could scarcely regard it as a sport.

Through a backward glance, we can imagine men of means using their general utility boats for harbor sails to shoot a brace of ducks or catch a mess of fish, with a possible friendly chase with another like-minded boater on their way to home port.

New York and Boston have the distinction of being the cities in which America's first pleasure boat sailing clubs were founded. Their amateur sailors had the vision to start organized yacht sailing. The Boston Yacht Club was founded in 1835; its only commodore was Captain Robert Bennet Forbes, who humorously dubbed the assemblage of old Boston sailors the "Dream Club" in honor of the club's flagship, the little schooner *Dream*. Forbes's club did not survive for long, while John C. Stevens's New York Yacht Club has endured.

Not only have the New York and Boston clubs the honor of founding organized pleasure boat sailing in America, but also they were the first to take up competitive yacht racing in a lively brush between Stevens's schooner, the *Wave*, and Forbes's schooner, the *Sylph*, in Vineyard Sound on August 3, 1835.

When an invitation from the Royal Yacht Squadron arrived on these shores for America to send over to England one of its fast pilot boats to the International Exposition of 1851, Stevens took the invitation as a personal challenge. Thus, Stevens was inspired to build the yacht *America*.

An example of a small nineteenth-century American coasting yacht from *Coasting Magazine*, July 1890.

The result of the August 22, 1851 race around the Isle of Wight is well known, so I will not repeat the details here. However, I will relate this interesting anecdote published in the September 1930 issue of the *Sketch Book Magazine*:

*The day after the* America *had launched a new era in yachting, building and design Queen Victoria and her husband, both of whom had seen part of the race, visited her. As Commodore Stevens was handing the young monarch down the companionway, the Prince Consort was sternly ordered by Captain Brown to wipe his royal feet. "I guess you don't know who I am," said the Prince. "I don't give a damn who you are, you'll wipe your feet before you go down into my cabin," was the old skipper's bluff reply. In addition, when the cabin was gained, the Queen was discovered wiping off the shelves to find a speck of dust. A gold compass with a letter from Her Majesty, expressing the hope that he would keep it as neat as he had the* America, *was Captain Brown's reward for what the world places next to godliness.*

Stevens brought the Cup back to New York, and after narrowly escaping being melted into six medals, it was finally formally deeded to the New York Yacht Club as a perpetual international sailing trophy. All foreign yacht clubs received notice of the dedication, but this failed to arouse any immediate interest. In the turmoil of the American Civil War, the Cup was forgotten; it lay for years in the closet of a home on Washington Square, New York, not unloved but certainly neglected.

Nearly two decades passed before England made an effort to regain the Cup and reestablish its yachting stature. Thus, rescued from obscurity, the celebrated Cup now sails the seas and resides, from time to time, in the halls of the world's most prestigious yacht clubs.

## Chapter 1

# THE YACHT *AMERICA*

The year 1851 was when the first International Fair took place. England intended the industries of the island nation to be displayed to the world. The Royal Yacht Squadron planned its annual regatta as a show of Britain's maritime superiority. An invitation went out across the Atlantic that all comers were welcome to enter the race.

The New York Yacht Club's commodore, John C. Stevens, commissioned James Rich Steers and George Steers to build a 170-ton schooner along the lines of the American pilot boat to send to the exposition; thus, the yacht *America* came into being.

The race was over the usual squadron course, with no time allowance. The start began from moorings, and fourteen British boats of all sizes and rigs went over the course.

A three-masted schooner of 392 tons, the *Brilliant*, was in the assembly, along with six schooners and seven sloops. The smallest contestant was the 47-ton sloop the *Aurora*. The *America* was slow in slipping her mooring and started last of the fleet. During the grueling race, the pod of racers witnessed the American boat steadily passing all competitors and arriving at the finish twenty-four minutes ahead of the second boat, the *Aurora*, and three hours and forty-six minutes before the *Brilliant*.

An interesting footnote to the *America*'s visit to England is that many believed she had a hidden propeller. Reversal of the belief came only after she was seen in dry dock.

The *America*'s career in British waters under the American flag was brief but profitable.

Commodore Stevens received many challenges to race the *America*; he ignored all until the *Titanla*, more adventuress than the others, challenged her. He agreed to a race for stakes of £100. On August 28, 1851, the *Titanla* was embarrassed by a loss of fifty-two minutes.

This decisive win netted the *America*'s owners $500, which so further enhanced her value that the syndicate was unable to resist an offer of $25,000 for a boat that cost $20,000. The trip to England cost $3,750; the six owners divided $1,750. This is the only recorded instance in which a yacht sailing for the Blue Ribbon of the seas paid a dividend.

The claim that the *America* was less swift than the British boats received some support when she passed into British hands and was soundly defeated.

The *America*'s new owner, Englishman John de Blaquiere, Second Baron de Blaquiere, raced her only a few times. Her mast was lowered and her rig altered with corresponding loss of speed. Blaquiere sold her in 1856 to Henry Montagu Upton, Second Viscount Templetown, who renamed the yacht *Camilla* but failed to use or maintain her. After an uneventful season, she was laid up at Cowes for five years, stuck in the mud flats where her timbers rotted.

In 1858, she was sold as junk to Henry Sotheby Pitcher. Pitcher, a shipbuilder in Gravesend, Kent, rebuilt *Camilla* and resold her in 1860 to Henry Edward Decie, who brought her back to the United States. Decie, a Confederate sympathizer, sold the ship to the Confederate States of America the same year for use as a blockade runner in the Civil War, and Decie remained her captain. During this time, she may have been renamed *Memphis*, but the details are unclear. In 1862, she was chased up the St. Johns River, where she was scuttled at Jacksonville to prevent capture when Union troops took the city.

After the war, she was raised, restored and again called *America* when she became a training ship for midshipmen at Annapolis.

The next notable event in the career of the *America* was her sale in 1870 to General Benjamin Franklin Butler, a former Civil War combatant, for $5,000. Butler and his family used her for cruising out of Boston for many years. In 1881, on her second cruise to the Caribbean, she sustained damage on Brigantine Shoals that necessitated rebuilding. Butler raced and maintained the boat well, commissioning a rebuild to Donald McKay in 1875 and a total refit of the rig to Edward Burgess in 1885 to keep her competitive. Upon the general's death in 1893, his son Paul inherited the schooner, but he had no interest in her and gave her to his nephew Butler Ames in 1897. Ames reconditioned the *America* and used her occasionally for racing and casual sailing until 1901, when she fell into disuse and disrepair.

In this August 23, 1967 photo, the *Intrepid* sails past a West Boothbay, Maine–built replica of the schooner *America* during the America's Cup trial races off Newport, Rhode Island.

The *America* was sold to a company headed by Charles H.W. Foster in 1917, and in 1921, she was sold to the *America* Restoration Fund. Again, the nation's love and respect for the old sailer prompted another restoration. Secretary of the Navy Charles Francis Adams began a fundraising drive from well-heeled private sources. Besides money from private donors, the yacht clubs of New Bedford and Fall River, Massachusetts, and New Haven and Stamford, Connecticut, as well as from the Newport Chamber of Commerce, each donated $200 to the restoration. Charles H.W. Foster gave the craft to the Eastern Yacht Club, which later sold her to the U.S. Naval Academy for $1 as the nucleus of an American maritime museum at Annapolis.

Lacking maintenance there, by 1940 she had become seriously decayed. On March 29, 1942, during a heavy snowstorm, the shed where the *America* was being stored collapsed. Three years later, in 1945, the remains of the shed and the ship were finally scrapped and burned.

*Chapter 2*

# BLUE RIBBON SAILORS

The evolution of the great racing machines that battle for the America's Cup, built for nothing but speed, is beautiful, costly and otherwise practically useless.

Racing large oceangoing yachts is the most pure form of sport; it is honest, clean and manly. The commercial and gambling element is secondary to the principal reason for the sport.

The modern Cup racer, when she has won or lost the prize, is about the most useless object afloat. The object that represents an investment of millions of dollars that has reached the highest point of its efficiency—that has lost none of its beauty—simply remains so much scrap. Such is the penalty for building fine racing machines that have no other useful purpose. It is a mere shell, highly uncomfortable at best and too frail to stand much use without continual repair.

The Herreshoff-built *Defender*, a marvel in her races, was broken up to save as much of her as the junkman would buy; the *Columbia* eventually followed the *Defender*'s fate. The *Vigilant*, rigged as a yawl, was the first Cup defender in which lightness took priority over strength and stability but to a lesser extent than in the latest boats.

The spectacle of these superb nineteenth-century racing machines makes one forget their utilitarian worthlessness. With a bronze underbody like

*Opposite page, from top to bottom*: The 1893 defender the *Vigilant* on dry dock; the 1893 British challenger the *Valkyrie II* on dry dock; the 1885 challenger *Genesta* on dry dock; and the 1885 Cup defender *Puritan* on dry dock.

The Herreshoff-built *Defender*, which defeated the *Valkyrie III* in the 1895 match.

burnished gold, the finely tuned hull seems a tiny thing under the press of snowy acres of canvas. Their majestic flight around the outer mark, with green sea white with froth boiling along the lee rail as the yachts come about, the furling or setting of spinnaker and jib, is to all who love the sea one of the most beautiful and exciting sights to behold.

The late 1800s 90-footers were triumphs of scientific marine engineering; mathematics took the place of the rule of thumb, and steel and bronze replaced oak and pine spar. It is not wise to believe that the huge racers were the product of the late nineteenth century; the gargantuan *Maria*, designed in 1844 by Robert Livingston Stevens for John C. Stevens, was 110 feet in overall length, her beam 26 feet, 8 inches, and 70 feet long on the boom. She carried only one headsail, a jib.

As a flyer, the *Maria* was certainly the fastest in her class; she logged seventeen nautical miles an hour. But she was fast in smooth water only; she was not a good sea boat.

The ideal craft of the day was the American pilot boat, the staunchest, speediest craft of her size in the world. The *America* belonged to that class. She was undoubtedly the best yacht of her time, but still British yachtsmen maintain that in the memorable race around the Isle of Wight when the *America* won the celebrated Cup, her triumph was not conclusive because the best English yacht, the *Arrow*, went aground.

Another Herreshoff-built flyer, the *Columbia*, which successfully defended the Cup in 1901 against the *Shamrock II*.

The schooner *Madeleine* is leading the *Countess of Dufferin* in the second race of the 1876 match. This was the last Cup race sailed in schooners.

Some in the yachting fraternity say if there is a worse course for a fair test of the merits of yachts than that of the Isle of Wight, it has not been found.

When the New York Yacht Club accepted a challenge for the Cup from the Canadian Major Gifford and his *Countess of Dufferin* in early 1876, the club committee made a proposal to the owners of the five most successful schooners in its fleet— the *Palmer*, the *Columbia*, the *Tidal Wave*, the *Madeleine* and the *Idler*—for a competition to choose the defender. Only the last two boats met for a match, and the centerboard schooner *Madeleine* won the honor of defending the Cup.

## THE SLOOP AND THE CUTTER

The three great eras in early American yachting were those of the *America*, which began in 1851 and ended in 1876; the advent of the cutter type, which dates from the American centennial year; and the period that dates from the advent of the *Defender* when the centerboard, the backbone and foundation of early American yacht designing, was abandoned.

The appearance of the Scottish cutter the *Kitten*, a boat designed by John Harvey of Wivenhoe, was largely responsible for the cutter enthusiasm. Unlike many fashions, it was a most admirable one. The distinction between cutter and sloop lies in the rig; however, the original meaning changed so that the term "cutter" came to stand for a deep, narrow craft with a keel and the term "sloop" for a wide, shallow vessel with a centerboard.

The cutter originated at Wivenhoe, on the muddy Colne in Essex, where England's best yachting skippers and sailors hailed. Most notable among the men whose names echoed in the sailors' public houses are Philip Sainty and his brother. The Saintys built swift smugglers with such speed that the revenue vessels were quickly lost from sight. Eventually, the Sainty brothers were caught and incarcerated. They languished in prison until the Marquis of Anglesey secured their pardon because he wanted a yacht that could beat the Duke of York's boat. In 1820, the Sainty boys built him the cutter *Pearl*, which outraced everything that challenged her.

The sloop is a product of Newburyport, Massachusetts, and this type of craft was more or less the standard in colonial America because Britain forbade the construction of any other type of vessel.

The shallow bays with which American coasts abound, especially around New York, produced a type of yacht, light of draft and broad

Herreshoff's bronze sloop the *Vigilant* is passing the *Valkyrie II* as the latter splits her third spinnaker during the October 13, 1893 match.

of beam, particularly suitable for estuarial cruising. However, there was a notable difference in the accepted types of schooners and sloops. The schooners were used chiefly for deep-sea cruising because a smaller crew could handle them, and as sailing about in shoal water was not felt to be desirable for them, they were built of deeper draft and less beam in proportion to their length. Thus, there were many keel schooners—for example, the *America*, the *Dauntless* and the *Sappho*—while prior to 1882, a keel sloop was almost unknown. In that year, several single stickers, built on the model of the English cutters, made their American appearance, but they usually failed to win races with only one or two exceptions.

The big sloops that won races and high esteem among yachtsmen were the *Fanny*, the *Mischief* and the *Gracie*, all beamy, light-draft, centerboard yachts.

Of these three sloops, the *Fanny* represented the extreme "skimming dish" and the *Gracie* a moderate use of beam with greater draft. In light breezes and smooth water, the *Fanny* usually took the prize, while in strong winds and rough seas the *Gracie* invariably won the race. The *Mischief*, midway between the two, was a dangerous adversary in light or moderate weather.

Each country developed the type of craft to meet local conditions. British waters are deep and stormy with choppy seas, while along the American coasts the seas are shallow with long, smooth swells in most weather. Still today, British and American boats sail best in their own waters.

In this October 1895 Punch cartoon, Uncle Sam is telling John Bull, "Say, John, you'd better go into training again!"

*Chapter 3*

# THE RACING MACHINES

Many who study the sport write that had the English sent large cutters as challengers in the 1885 and 1886 races, they would have taken the Cup. When *Yankee* designers saw the fine showing by the Scottish cutter *Madge* in American waters, they realized the value of the cutter rig and appropriated it along with the cutter stern, though they adhered to the centerboard.

Realistically speaking, owing to the British measurement system, the English cutter of that day was far from a perfect craft. Many of the wonderful things associated with yacht design are due to the marine architects' effort to defeat the rules by which racing committees compute a boat's size in order to fix the handicap it must allow to smaller competitors.

English designers during the mid- to late nineteenth century found that boat length was cheap and there was no price on depth, while beam "was heavily taxed." The result was a long, deep and very narrow craft, "a plank on edge, with a lead mine underneath." These so-called tonnage cheaters were very fast and strong in heavy winds.

Latter-day handicappers suggest that if Sir William Sutton had challenged with the *Genesta* in 1882 instead of 1885, he very likely would have captured the Cup. The first real struggle between single stickers began with the *Genesta-Puritan* contest in 1885. The defender *Puritan*, built by Edward Burgess, who incorporated many British ideas, was the largest sloop built since the *Maria*. She had the beam and power of a Yankee sloop with the outside lead of an English cutter and a slot keel through which the

The Edward Burgess–designed *Mayflower* is leading the *Galaten* in the second race of the 1886 match.

centerboard worked. She was without a doubt the fastest of any boat built in America up to that time, yet she beat the *Genesta* by only a little more than a minute and a half in a twenty-mile race to leeward and return.

To meet Lieutenant William Henn's 1886 challenge, the flag offices of the New York Yacht Club ordered an enlarged and improved *Mischief.* Until this year, Boston had taken no part in the Cup's defense, but a syndicate of ten members of the Eastern Yacht Club headed by Civil War general Charles J. Paine[1] financed construction of W. Starling Burgess's *Yankee.*

J. Beavor-Webb designed both the *Genesta* and Lieutenant Henn's *Galaten*, which challenged the next year. The *Galaten* was pronounced an improvement on her predecessor, but she proved a total disappointment, while in the *Mayflower*, Burgess produced a faster boat than the *Puritan*, which easily defeated her. Now, the racing machine idea was beginning to take hold in yacht design circles; in the *Mayflower*'s specially lightened rigging is shown the new design influence.

On the night of his final defeat, Henn, in good spirit in spite of his loss, wanted to fill the Cup with wine, but Secretary Oddie, lifting the ten pounds of silver from the dining table of the club at 67 Madison Avenue, showed conclusively that the America's Cup "hath no bottom."

## THE BRITISH RACING MACHINE

When George L. Watson began planning a craft designed especially for American waters, it was the first time naval architecture was directed to win a certain series of races in certain waters and under certain probable conditions. The result of this design decision was the *Thistle*. She measured slightly less than ninety feet on the waterline and was a radical departure from her predecessors. Her beam was more than twenty feet.

The *Thistle* was the most handsome and fastest boat to come over seeking the Cup, but she was not fast enough to catch the *Volunteer*.

General Charles J. Paine of the New York Yacht Club contracted Edward Burgess to design his Cup defender the *Volunteer*, a centerboard sloop with an all-steel frame and hull and a deck of white pine, for the 1887 races. *Period stereo view photo.*

For the 1887 match, Edward Burgess was again consulted, and he turned out a masterpiece in the iron sloop *Volunteer*; entirely paid for by General Paine, she measured three feet shorter than the *Thistle* and three feet wider. Burgess broke from the straight stern in favor of the sharp, concave clipper bow. The *Volunteer* was a powerful boat, and it is doubtful if any boat could ever go to windward faster. She was more English than her predecessor was, just as the Scotch cutter *Thistle* was more American, but the advantage was with the Boston boat, and she won an overwhelming victory. The *Volunteer* showed her superiority at the very beginning of the first race (which she won) over the club course by nineteen minutes, twenty-three seconds, with an allowance of five seconds to her opponent. In the second race, sailed over a forty-mile ocean course with a beat to windward at the start, the *Volunteer* won the run home in a stiff breeze by a decisive margin of eleven minutes, forty-eight seconds, corrected time.

# Chapter 4

# THE 1893 AND 1895 MATCHES

Almost immediately after the 1887 contest, a challenge came from the Royal Clyde Yacht Club on behalf of Charles Sweet, but before negotiations could begin, the challenge was withdrawn.

After this came a pause in challenges, but in 1893, the Royal Yacht Squadron arranged a match with another Watson creation, the *Valkyrie II*, the haughty Lord Dunraven's cutter.[2] To meet this challenge, New York and Boston syndicates ordered two yachts each.

Since the last match, Edward Burgess had gone to his eternal reward, but a new star had arisen in naval architecture: the talented and ingenious Rhode Islander Captain Nathanael Greene Herreshoff. His unrivaled *Gloriana* was far superior to anything in her class in the 1891 season. Captain Nat possessed that rare talent of being able to create a boat of beautiful line imbued with the ability to win over all challengers.

The New York syndicates ordered two boats from Captain Nat—one of bronze, the centerboard *Vigilant,* and the other of steel, the keel craft *Colonia.* The Boston boats were also of steel—the *Jubilee,* designed by John B. Paine, the eldest son of General Paine, who once again single-handedly financed a Cup defender, and the other the *Pilgrim,* by the firm of Stewart and Binney.

The *Pilgrim,* built with steel throughout, the weight of her frames a bit heavier than some former defenders, was compensated with light plating. She received extra strength where extra strain was expected, with her deck strapping in the usual way. The steel plates were treated with muriatic acid

The Earl of Dunraven's yacht, the sleek and powerful *Valkyrie III*, posed a real threat to take the Cup. This extraordinary photo attests to her undisputable fouling of the *Defender*.

before they were applied to the frame. No reduction of speed was anticipated because of the lapping of the plates.

The *Pilgrim*'s overall length (LOA) was 120 feet, her waterline length (LWL) 85 feet, her beam 23 feet and her draft 5 feet. The fin measured 17 feet, 6 inches, so her full draft was 22 feet, 6 inches, with about twenty tons of lead ballast at the fin bottom.

The following quote from the October 14, 1893 weekly journal *Scientific American* is a sportswriter's description of the *Valkyrie II*:

> *The British yacht* Valkyrie [II] *that is to sail against the* Vigilant, *arrived at New York September 22, after the rather long voyage of thirty days from Southampton, England.*
>
> *She has a long, well shaped body, and looks to be a thorough racer. Her construction shows a radical departure from all English precedents. Her spar and sail plan are unlike anything before attempted by English designers. Her estimated dimensions are length over all, 120 feet; water line length, 85 feet; beam, 22 feet 6 inches; draught, 15 feet 6 inches; boom, 90 feet. Her bowsprit is only 16 feet long. Her mast is stepped well forward. In her races on the other side, the* Valkyrie [II] *has shown up better in light airs. She is strong to windward and fast on a reach. The harder it blows, the better she seems to like it.*

By 1893, the spoon bow had reached the big single-masted boats, and the long overhang meant a "measurement cheater." When the yacht heeled, those forty-five unmeasured feet became exceedingly valuable as a sailing floor.

The *Vigilant* was the first craft to have an underbody of Tobin bronze; this surface allowed her to slip through the water with the least amount of friction. Above the water, her weight was as light as possible, but she carried tremendous weight in her keel in order to bear the massive sail plan. Her hollow bronze centerboard could drop 10 feet; without the centerboard, her draft was 14 feet. This powerful craft was 130 feet over all, a fraction more than 86 feet of waterline and 26 feet abeam.

George J. Gould's yacht the *Vigilant* won the Goelet Cup[3] in the Newport, Rhode Island trials. She won the esteemed trophy because of the *Defender*'s bad luck. The *Defender* led all around the course and was only five miles from the finish when her gaff snapped just about the middle of the spar and she quit the race. The *Vigilant*'s victory of the trial races made her Cup defender.

The *Vigilant* successfully defended the Cup, defeating the *Valkyrie II* in three straight matches.

# Sailing to Victory

Like Ashbury twenty years earlier, Lord Dunraven refused to be discouraged and came back to an equally embarrassing defeat in 1895 with another Watson production, the *Valkyrie III*. For the 1895 challenge, the New York Yacht Club turned again to Herreshoff, who designed and built a composite boat, the *Defender*, which proved equal to the task of sinking the hopes of the British lord.

The weekly *Scientific American* of August 31, 1895, published the following anonymous sportswriter's description of the *Valkyrie III*:

> [Tuning] *trials, such as they are, would seem to show that* Valkyrie [III] *will be a very dangerous competitor in light breezes, and a very harmless one in a blow.*
>
> *The* Valkyrie [III] *is of what is known as composite construction—elm planking on nickel-steel frames. She is not coppered, except on her lead keel; but is painted with a patent enamel, which is said to give a remarkably smooth surface. She is more stoutly rigged than the* Defender *and is every way a heavier boat.*
>
> *Probably about 55 per cent of the displacement of the* Defender *is in her lead keel; for* Valkyrie [III] *the ratio will be about 50 per cent.*
>
> *It will be seen, from the above facts, that there is much about the coming struggle to make it especially exciting. It promises to be more evenly contested than any previous series of races.*

The *Defender* sailed alone in the final race of the ninth challenge on September 12, 1895, after *Valkyrie III* withdrew, complaining of interference by the spectator fleet. *Period stereo view photo.*

By this time, racing yachts had ceased being national types; they differed only as the ideas of the designers differed, and no more than boats planned by different men in America.

From the beginning of the Herreshoff Manufacturing Company, Herreshoff yachts were marked by lines so peculiarly his that it is impossible to confuse them with models of other builders. Herreshoff yachts are characterized by a long and full amidships section, moderate dead arise and a clean run, and the run and futtock timbers are invariably attached to the deadwood and keel almost at right angles, without any of the gentle, curved modeling or the hollow floor usual in foreign and most American vessels and carried to the furthest limit in the English lead-keeled cutter. These yachts are further characterized by a high freeboard and great sheer, both fore and aft, the forward curve, following a parabolic line, beginning about a third of the length from the stern.

Herreshoff abandoned the centerboard and for the 1895 match came out with the *Defender*, which critics said to be the most pure racing machine ever

The *Australia* skipper Jim Hardy and owner Alan Bond (right) acknowledge the cheers of well-wishers. The *Australia* team just defeated the Swedish entry, the *Sverige*, to win their division in the semifinal series to choose the Cup challenger. *UPI photo, Newport, Rhode Island, August 26, 1980.*

constructed. The *Defender* was all bronze and lead below the waterline and aluminum and steel above. She had a narrower beam than the *Vigilant*, while the challenger, *Valkyrie III*, was wider than her predecessors. More sail was crowded on the boats, and the factor of safety was cut to the minimum; the rallying cry of "Anything for speed!" was the motto.

The *Defender* won the first race, and in the second race, the *Valkyrie III* fouled the *Defender* and was disqualified. Just before the start of the third race, the *Valkyrie III* withdrew, complaining of interference by the large spectator fleet crowding the racecourse and powerboats crossing her beam. However, the *Defender* sailed the course and was declared the winner. Dunraven accused the Americans of adding or shifting the *Defender*'s ballast, creating a longer waterline. An investigation ensued in which Dunraven's claim was declared unfounded. Strong language was exchanged and led to Dunraven being expelled as an honorary member of the New York Yacht Club.

A review of the *Defender–Valkyrie III* races by a contemporary writer summed up the races as "a fluke, a foul, and a fizzle"—a commentary agreed to by many who witnessed the ignominious defeat and bad behavior of the challenger.

# Chapter 5

# BIOGRAPHICAL SKETCHES OF PRINCIPAL PLAYERS

## JOHN COX STEVENS

Stevens, founder of the New York Yacht Club, was also head of the syndicate that built the schooner *America*.

Stevens was the son of a Union army colonel. He and his inventive brothers are responsible for many innovative firsts. Together they developed steam gunboats for the U.S. Navy and operated a lucrative passenger and freight steamboat enterprise.

His undying devotion to everything American led him to build the *America*. His principal reason for sending his yacht to race the British was to display the supremacy of American shipbuilding and design. Unable

Commodore John C. Stevens's portrait from *Coasting Magazine*, July 1892.

to finance the campaign on his own, he formed a syndicate of five wealthy New York Yacht Club members to aid in constructing, rigging and sailing the yacht.

# LORD WINDHAM THOMAS WYNDHAM-QUIN

Lord Dunraven, the fourth Earl of Dunraven and Second Baron Kenry, challenged twice for the coveted Cup, first in 1893 and again in 1895.

As an amateur naval architect, Dunraven complained that he saw additional ballast being added to the *Defender* after final measurement and accused the Americans of cheating. A distinguished panel of New York Yacht Club members thought otherwise.

He insisted that the New York Yacht Club alter the conditions governing match races, which led to the Deed of Gift being redrafted. His arrogant insistence and bad manners led to the most acrimonious dispute in the Cup's distinguished history. Harsh words were exchanged, and Dunraven was expelled as an honorary member of the New York Yacht Club. C. Oliver Iselin,

The Earl of Dunraven was born in Ireland, educated at Oxford and served in the First Light Guards. He served as a diplomat under Lord Salisbury.

a great yachtsman and the brilliant manager of the *Vigilant*, the *Defender* and, later, the *Columbia*, played an important role in this controversy.

Unfortunately for Dunraven, he is remembered in yachting history as a quitter and bad sport.

# C. OLIVER ISELIN

C. Oliver Iselin's sailing career began with small, over-rigged boats known as sandbaggers. These were wide shoal boats on which overturning was always imminent. He raced catboats in Long Island Sound and gained a reputation as a keen racing skipper while still in his teens.

C. Oliver Iselin, an American yachtsman of Swiss descent, the son of the founder of A. Iselin & Co. and a member of many clubs, crewed on the Cup defender *Volunteer*. He later managed Captain Nat's *Reliance*.

Iselin, whose grandfather had amassed a large fortune in the importing business, gained membership to the New York Yacht Club in 1877. Within ten years, he found himself a crew member aboard the *Volunteer*. This experience no doubt led to Iselin's successful management of the Cup yachts built by the Herreshoff Manufacturing Company. He headed up the *Vigilant* syndicate in 1893, the same year the Earl of Dunraven was elected to the New York Yacht Club as an honorary member.

Aboard the *Defender* in the 1895 Cup challenge, Iselin was at the center of the Earl of Dunraven controversy.

In 1899, Iselin managed the syndicate that built the Herreshoff yacht *Columbia* at an astonishing cost of $250,000. Coming out of retirement to manage the *Reliance* in 1903, Iselin oversaw a perfect defense that year. As manager of these Cup defender syndicates, he showed the embodiment of America's Cup spirit. He understood the great yachts, commanded with authority and defended the America's Cup with honor and dignity.[4]

## SIR THOMAS JOHNSTONE LIPTON

The humble origin of the world's most wealthy tea merchant is akin to a rags-to-riches story out of a Dickens novel.

Born in Glasgow, son of an Irish day laborer, Lipton, through a unique style of shopkeeping and imaginative advertising, grew a small grocery store into an international business. In 1899, at the age of thirty, the year of his first attempt to win the Cup, his fortune was estimated at $20 million.

Although a member of the Royal Ulster Yacht Club, Lipton was not a yachtsman. His five Cup challenges awakened lethargic marine sporting men from many maritime nations. His first *Shamrock* challenge in 1899 and his continued resolve to sail his *Shamrock* yachts to victory in 1901, 1903, 1920 and 1930 were said to be due to his unquenchable thirst to keep the name Lipton before the eyes of the world.

Pursued by many women on both sides of the Atlantic, Lipton remained a lifelong bachelor. He was knighted in 1898 and became a baronet in 1902; he was elected to the Royal Yacht Squadron in 1931. He continued to be respected for his courteous demeanor and sportsmanship as, one by one, all five of the *Shamrocks* were defeated.

## SIR THOMAS OCTAVE MURDOCK SOPWITH

Sopwith, a pioneer in aviation, made two challenges for the Cup in his J-class yachts in 1934 with the *Endeavour* and in 1937 with the *Endeavour II*.

Sopwith brought his aeronautical precision into his yacht racing; his novel electric wind instruments and backstay tension-measuring devices brought modern innovations to the sport. He was an avid and seasoned sailor. As an owner who skippered his boats and had his wife sail with him as timekeeper, he was to some extent a rarity for those days. Only his lack

Thomas O.M. Sopwith began flying airplanes in 1910 at age forty-nine; he began building planes in 1912 and made a fortune selling them during World War II. He took up yachting in 1928.

In the late 1970s, Ted Hood had more influence on America's Cup matches sailed in twelve-meter yachts than any person involved in the sailboat-rigging industry.

of tactical ability in a race caused him to lose his grip on the Cup, which was within his grasp when he had the faster boat in 1934.

Many readers will remember stories of the remarkable World War I biplane the Sopwith Camel and the swift British fighter of World War II, the Hawker Siddeley.

# TED HOOD

Ted Hood, an engineer and naval architect, owned a sail-making company that developed the Dacron cloth from which the twelve-meter sails are cut. He designed his Cup defense candidates for the 1964 and 1977 races.

The 1974 defense built two aluminum boats; the R. McCullough syndicate financed the *Courageous* designed by Olin Stephens and the *Mariner* by Britton Chase. The *Mariner*'s radical new design was not the hoped-for breakthrough. The W.J. Strawbridge syndicate sponsored the wood *Intrepid*'s rebuild close to her original lines after her modification for the 1970 match.

Hood won the Cup when he managed the *Courageous* in 1974.

# BILL FICKER

As the saying goes, "Ficker Is Quicker."

In 1970, the California architect proved to be the better skipper when he sailed the *Intrepid* to a successful defense of the Cup. With superior tactics and a dedicated crew who perfected the boat and its sails, he won on what is generally thought of as the slower boat.

Universally considered a brilliant organizer, he devoted great effort to training his crew. He admitted that his success in winning races was by letting his navigator and tactician have free rein. With this approach, he could concentrate his efforts on producing the best possible speed from the altered Olin Stephens–designed *Intrepid* and ensure he made not a single mistake.

# OLIN J. STEPHENS

Stephens shares the record with Nat Herreshoff of designing six America's Cup defenders. Largely self-taught, he started his career by designing several successful day-sailers and then built the *Dorade*, with which he and his brother Rod won the 1931 transatlantic race by two days.

Olin and Rod got their first taste of America's Cup racing in 1934, an experience that was of great help later in perfecting their designs. In 1937, Olin and Starling Burgess designed the *Ranger*, the last J-boat to defend the America's Cup.

Olin Stephens was co-designer of the *Ranger* with W. Starling Burgess. He is known throughout the world for his winning yacht designs.

She was also the first defender since the *Volunteer* in 1887 not built by the Herreshoff Manufacturing Company.

The *Ranger* was huge and powerful, easily defeating the *Endeavour* in four straight races. She won thirty-two of thirty-four races by an average of seven minutes. Olin Stephens served as tactician on the *Ranger*, while his brother Rod was deck boss. The fact that they were crack sailors helped them immeasurably when they joined with Drake Sparkman to form Sparkman & Stephens.

Recognizing the end of the J-boat era, Vanderbilt commissioned Sparkman & Stephens to design his first twelve-meter yacht in 1939. The highly respected marine architect was first to realize the benefits of tank testing scale models of his designs. With the aid of the newly installed model test tank at Stevens Institute in Hoboken, New Jersey, Stephens designed the *Vim*, a boat that won twenty-one of her twenty-seven starts against the best of the International twelve-meter fleet in 1939. Nineteen years later, the *Vim* gave the *Columbia*, another Stephens-designed twelve-meter, all she could handle before losing the final America's Cup trial series by only twelve seconds. The average winning margin in the *Vim-Columbia* series, called the best set of match races ever sailed, was only thirty-two seconds.

Olin Stephens later became the designer of practically all the twelve-meter America's Cup defenders, including the *Columbia* and the *Constellation* in 1964, the *Intrepid* in 1967, the *Courageous* in 1974 and the *Freedom* in 1980. The most noted yacht designer of his era, his boats are winners throughout the world.

Stephens's 1938 twelve-meter yacht *Vim* set a new standard in the class and stood a chance to defend in 1958. The refurbished *Vim* raced in trials against his *Columbia*, which narrowly beat out the twenty-year-old boat and successfully defended the Cup. His winning defenders include the *Constellation* in 1964, the *Intrepid* in 1967, the *Courageous* in 1974 and 1977 and the *Freedom* in 1980.[5]

# ROBERT E. "TED" TURNER III

Advertising and media mogul Ted Turner, alternately called the "Mouth from the South" and "Captain Courageous," was born in Cincinnati, Ohio. The family moved to Atlanta when he was nine. He attended MacCallie Military School in Chattanooga, Tennessee. According to Dennis Conner, "He went from being the worst cadet to the best. He was singled out as the 'neatest cadet' in his junior year. The worst and the best remain Turner's salient personality traits to this day."

Turner is credited with the invention of the spinnaker chute in the Flying Dutchman class. With his purchase of the failed twelve-meter America's Cup yacht *American Eagle* converted into an ocean racer, he compiled a record unmatched in ocean racing, winning the World Ocean Racing Championship in 1970.

He is notorious for being loud on the water; most of his bluster is in a form used to psych up his crews to make them feel good about what they are doing and to give them a purpose to hustle. He was involved in three Cup-defense campaigns: as skipper in the 1974 defender trials with the *Mariner* and twice with the *Courageous* (in 1977, when he successfully defended the Cup, and in 1980, when he was beat in the trials by Dennis Conner and the *Freedom*).

# Sir James Gilbert Hardy

Wealthy British-born New South Wales viticultor Sir James Gilbert Hardy, called "Gentleman Jim" because of his impeccable manners, became involved with America's Cup match racing when, in 1967, he crewed on the *Gretel* when she was a trial horse to the *Dame Pattie*.

For the 1970 Cup races, three challenges were received from abroad—one from Australia, one from Sweden and one from France. For this situation, the New York Yacht Club allowed the multiple challengers to hold a series of races to select the challenger.

In 1970, Hardy skippered the Australian *Gretel II* in the first-ever challenger selection races against Baron Marcel Bick's yacht the *France* and Sweden's entry the *Sverige*, defeating both and becoming the challenger of record.

Alan Bond chose Hardy as helmsman for his boat the *Southern Cross* in the 1974 match against the *Courageous*, skippered by Dennis Conner.

Hardy returned to Newport in 1977 to skipper Bond's new stallion, the *Australia*. The *Australia* defeated the *Gretel II*, the *France* and Sweden's *Sverige* in the challenger selection races but lost the Cup to Ted Turner's *Courageous*.

## Dennis Conner

Dennis Conner was born on September 16, 1942, in San Diego, California, just one block from the San Diego Yacht Club; as a boy, he began sailing with his father, a commercial fisherman. Conner, being a likable youngster, earned the friendship of many local yacht owners and skippers who mentored the lad. After graduating from a local public school, Conner went on to study at San Diego State University, always sailing in his spare time. His early financial foundation included ownership of Vera's Draperies, Carpet and Drapery Manufactory and retail sales.

Dennis Conner successfully defended the America's Cup in 1974, 1980 and 1988 and won as the challenger in 1987 after his historic loss in 1983 to Alan Bond's wing-keeled challenger *Australia II*. As helmsman of the first Cup defender to be defeated in the 132-year history of the Cup, Conner said, "In my heart, I knew I had done everything I could."

In 1987, Conner formed his own syndicate and raced for the San Diego Yacht Club. In that year's match races, Conner outsailed Australian defender the *Kookaburra III* four wins to naught in the best-of-seven series, bringing the Cup back to America.

Dennis Conner guides his twelve-meter yacht the *Liberty* to the starting line in the 1983 defender-selection series. *AP laser photo.*

From 1987 through 2003, Conner skippered his celebrated *Stars & Stripes* yachts. Within the yachting community, Conner is most famous for fundamentally changing America's Cup racing in general from an amateur to professional status. Before the 1980s, America's Cup competitors were principally amateur sailors. Conner insisted on year-round training with a new focus on physical fitness and practice. This change in approach led to a return to the 1930s type of professional crews in sailing.

In 1988, Conner defeated New Zealand banker Michael Fay's controversial maxiboat. Fay's team challenged with his ninety-foot super-sloop the *New Zealand* (KZ1). Conner's San Diego Yacht Club responded with a sixty-foot wing-sail catamaran, the *Stars & Stripes* (US-1), in a surprise defense, winning 2–0.

Fay's challenge and legal case based on the Deed of Gift foreshadowed the controversial Thirty-third America's Cup race, whose legal wrangling resulted in the contest being sailed in enormous multihull crafts in February 2010, returning to the prewar style of exclusive, billionaire-backed campaigns like those of the *Alinghi* and the *BMW Oracle*.

Dennis Conner is a maker of America's Cup history. In addition to being the first to skipper a boat in five America's Cup matches, Conner is also the first skipper in Cup history to sail the defender trials on one boat and the match on another. To Conner's regret, he is also the only defending skipper to lose the Cup twice.

# Alan Bond

It took Alan Bond, a sign and house painter and real estate developer, to wrest the America's Cup from the New York Yacht Club. In 1983, in his fourth and final attempt to take the Cup, he succeeded with a professional crew and the innovative winged-keel on his *Australia II*. Bond's fourth challenge, by its success, changed the face of yachting history.

A modern rags-to-riches story, at age twenty-nine, in 1967, Bond made his first million. As a hobby to help him relax, Bond took up ocean sailing. His first sailboat was the *Panamuna*, taken as a swap for a piece of real estate. After destroying two masts, he scrapped the *Panamuna* and contracted Bob Miller to design a new boat, a fifty-eight-footer called *Apollo*. In 1970, Bond and Miller brought the *Apollo* to Newport to race in the Newport–Bermuda race. Coincidentally, while preparing the *Apollo* for the race at Robert E. Derecktor's boatyard, Dennis Conner's trial horse, the twelve-meter *Valiant*, was being built there. Bond, Miller and his crew wandered over to view the *Valiant* and were told clearly that they should leave the area.

Dennis Conner, in his 1998 book,[6] tells of the face-to-face this way:

> *Miller, a bear of a man, responded that they weren't interested "in your bloody Cup or boat. If we were we'd come back and win it." Four years later, they were back. Less than 10 years after that, in 1983, they suited deeds to words, by winning it—the first time that had happened in 132 years.*

As Neil Armstrong's one huge step advanced humankind, so has Alan Bond's tenacity resulted in one huge step forward for Australia.

## JOHN BERTRAND

Bertrand is the man who skippered the boat that won the Cup for the Royal Perth Yacht Club. He is an engineer who studied the aerodynamics of twelve-meter sails. In the 1970 challenge, he received his first sailing experience aboard the *Gretel II* as a trimmer and came back with Bond aboard the *Southern Cross* in 1974. He learned early in his sailing career that intensive concentration is required on the water because twelves are difficult boats to sail well.

Bond's choice of Bertrand as his skipper and helmsman on the *Australia II* was a natural one. He sailed in four Cup campaigns on twelve-meters and was an experienced ocean racer.

The obsession of winning the Cup is in his genes; his great-grandfather was involved with Lipton's *Shamrock* challenges. One may say Bertrand was born to win the America's Cup, which he did with class and changed yachting history.

## WILLIAM INGRAHAM KOCH

Wichita, Kansas native Bill Koch is the son of Fred C. Koch, founder of Koch Industries, a business empire founded on oil refining, which became the largest privately owned company in America. He attended Culver Military Academy in Culver, Indiana, and graduated from the Massachusetts Institute of Technology with a degree in engineering. Working in his family's company, he eventually became a part owner, but he later sold his share to his brothers, Charles and David. He is the founder and president of the Oxbow Group, an energy development holding company based in West Palm Beach, Florida.

Koch is an avid supporter of the Sea Scout program of the Boy Scouts of America, biannually hosting the William I. Koch International Sea Scout Cup.

Shortly after the New York Court of Appeals issued its ruling in 1990 that awarded the America's Cup to the San Diego Yacht Club, multimillionaire Bill Koch burst on the scene with his mantra of technology, teamwork and talent and the most massive war chest ever. He contracted his initial racing yacht in 1990 at Hercules Aerospace Industries in Magna, Utah, a builder of rocket engines and NASA Space Transportation System (space shuttle) parts. The yacht called *Jayhawk* raced in the World's Whitebread competition. At the competition, the *Jayhawk* joined Koch's *USA2*, the former French yacht that the America³ syndicate purchased from the obsolete Beach Boys syndicate. This older boat, renamed *America³*, stayed at the back of the fleet, while the *Jayhawk*'s performance was disappointing.

Later, the America³ syndicate sold the *USA2* back to the French and concentrated on building the syndicate's second yacht. Doug Peterson, Jim Pugh and John Reichel (an expatriate from the Beach Boys syndicate) joined the America³ syndicate; their original design principles were incorporated in the second boat, named *Defiant*, built at the Eric Goetz boat yard in Bristol, Rhode Island.

The combination proved unbeatable as the rookie, who insisted on frequently steering his own boat, showed the veterans how to build a fast sailboat. His new *America³* first dispatched Dennis Conner and then surprised most America's Cup pundits when he won the 1992 America's Cup with his Bristol-built yacht, the *America³*, defeating the Italian *Il Moro di Venezia* four races to one.

The *America³*'s overall record including trials was 28-10. Koch reportedly went on a four-yacht spending spree of around $65 million on his effort to defend the America's Cup; an amateur, he sailed on the crew himself, assisted by veteran helmsman Buddy Melges.

He donated the *Jayhawk*, one of the four boats he used in qualifying for the America's Cup defense, to the Wichita Boathouse and another yacht, the *Defiant*, to the Herreshoff Marine Museum and America's Cup Hall of Fame. In 1995, Koch financed another team to defend for the Cup. This time, the crew consisted entirely of women, except for tactician David Dellenbaugh, on a yacht named *Mighty Mary*. However, the boat lost to Dennis Conner's *Stars & Stripes* in the trials.

The launch of the *Constitution*; a lithograph from the *Graphic*, an illustrated weekly London newspaper, May 25, 1901.

*Chapter 6*

# THE LIPTON CAMPAIGNS

One of the most interesting figures in international yachting came on the scene in 1899 in the person of Sir Thomas Johnstone Lipton, a wealthy Irish tea merchant; his was the voracious desire to return the Cup to the British Isles.

Turning first to one designer and then to another, Sir Tom ordered boat upon boat without hesitation. Being the solitary financial backer of each boat, he never interfered in their management once they were in commission, and he never sailed on any of them in a Cup race. His persistence, however, won for him the reputation of being a great yachtsman and sporting gentleman, although he readily admitted that he never held the wheel of a yacht in a race.

All five Lipton challenges came by way of the Royal Ulster Yacht Club of Belfast, Ireland, and all five yachts, over a period of thirty-one years, were named *Shamrock*, with the usual Roman numeral after the first.

At the launching of Lipton's first yacht, Lady Russell christened her *Shamrock*. There was no doubt of the interest and excitement at her coming out, though every attempt to belittle her was made by the disgruntled Dunraven camp. Lipton said, "We have engaged to win back the America's Cup. We have fairly extended ourselves, and if we are beaten, all I can say is, honor to the yacht which is better than the *Shamrock*."

The *Shamrock*'s designer, William Fife Jr., said, "Brains and all that careful thought and knowledge of naval architecture can put into a yacht are there. Every man of us is satisfied that with a fair field we shall give a tight race to any opponent."

*Above*: The enclosure at the yard of Denny Brothers at Dumbarton, near Glasgow, in which the *Shamrock II* was built.

*Below*: The launching of the *Shamrock II*, April 20, 1901. Because of the shallowness of the cove, her introduction to the sea is on a pontoon.

High hopes reign at such a time. The *Shamrock* had all the points of a strong competitor, so there was reason to look forward to a close series of contests for the Cup that year.

Again, an appeal, this time by Commodore J. Pierpoint Morgan, reached Nat Herreshoff for a defender, and the answer was the bronze sloop *Columbia*, considered by many the fastest single-masted vessel ever built. Fife's *Shamrock* was easily defeated in the first and third races; she withdrew from the second after losing her topmast.

# SHAMROCK *II*

Two years later, William Watson produced the *Shamrock II*. Watson tried to produce a yacht with the essential features of the American racers, but his work was largely experimental. Before this, the typical English racing cutter was a long, narrow, deep vessel. She kept from rolling over by an immense weight of lead bolted to her keel. She was slow in light air because she had so much body under water and so little sail above. She was fast and could go smartly about her business in a choppy blow.

Off Sandy Hook during the yachting season, there are seldom heavy winds or rough seas. Moderate to brisk winds prevail, and the sea is smooth or runs in long swells. The design of American yachts of those early days was for such conditions as these.

The *Shamrock II* is seen in 1902 on a British real photo postcard.

The 1901 Cup defender the *Columbia* trumped the *Shamrock II* challenger in three straight races. *Period stereo view photo.*

The problems facing designers of racing yachts are the increase of sail carrying power and the decrease of the resistance of the hull in passing through the water. Sail carrying power is obtained, first, by giving a yacht plenty of beam. It is increased by giving her depth and placing the ballast at the lowest point. Resistance to the water is diminished by making the part of the vessel that is under water as small as possible. To accomplish this, designers cut away the forward part of the underbody of their vessels so that the whole bow is nothing but a long, narrow blade. Then they raise the bilge, the shoulder formed at the point where the inward and downward curve of the side begins, as high as possible. A deep keel, with some ninety tons of lead at its extreme lower edge, completes the design.

Both the *Columbia* and the *Shamrock II* show all these features. The only difference between the two antagonists is in the proportion of length to breadth.

The *Columbia* managed to repeat her earlier defeat of the *Shamrock*, although her margin in the last race was only forty-one seconds.

## SHAMROCK *III*

In the 1903 match, another Herreshoff creation, the 143-foot giant the *Reliance*, the largest of the Cup-defending sloops with a sail area of 16,000 square feet, soundly defeated the third *Shamrock*.

The elegant flyer the *Shamrock III* preparing for the 1903 Cup races. *Period postcard image.*

A dramatic study of the handsome *Reliance* sailing toward the wind. *Period postcard image.*

The measurements alone of the third Lipton challenger would stand out as distinct from any of the recent yachts that had crossed the Atlantic to do battle for the celebrated Cup. Until then, the challengers, with the possible exception of the *Valkyrie III*, designed by George L. Watson, had followed a distinct line of development, tracing the progress from one to the other and the efforts made in each succeeding boat to make good the apparent weaknesses of her predecessors. In the bold bid the *Shamrock II* made for success in her contest with the *Columbia,* William Fife had in his designing of the *Shamrock III* strong temptation to follow the same lines. However, inspection of the new boat before the hour planned for her launch showed that Fife had chosen to return some very essential features to the type of model of the *Britannia,* whose successful defeat of the *Vigilant* led to the embodiment by Herreshoff of *Britannia*'s lines, greatly refined in the *Defender.*

It has long been a conviction among designers that the time allowance given for lack of waterline length does not put the shorter boat on a level with the yacht of greater length, and their desire has therefore been to build as near the allowable limit of 90 feet as possible. The *Shamrock III* was within a few inches of the limit, but in the matter of overall length, which goes untaxed, the new challenger was more than any Cup yacht yet built. Forward, her overhang measured 25 feet, and a similar length in the bow brought her total length from stem to stern to 140 feet.

# Sailing to Victory

When the underbody of the *Shamrock III* was revealed in dry dock at the Erie Basin, it corresponded very closely with the description furnished by an American spy assigned by the weekly journal *Scientific American* to view the launching.

In one paragraph, the anonymous author of an April 25, 1903 *Scientific American* article sums up the expectations of many concerning the American defender soon to face the British challenger:

> *The events of the yachting seasons of 1901 and 1902, and the performance of certain very successful racing craft in those two years, notably the Cup yacht* Independence, *and the sister boats* Neola *and* Weetamoe, *which more than saved their time on the Herreshoff 70-footers last year, rendered it pretty certain in the judgment of the yachting "sharpies" that, when the folding doors of the Herreshoff building shed were opened, there would pass out through them a vessel of very exaggerated proportions of the forward and after overhang of the new boat, as shown they are the work of such cautious and conservative builders as the Bristol firm.*

We learn the following from the *Scientific American* dated June 27, 1903:

> Shamrock III *is a marked departure, in some respects, from any challenger that has been sent over from the other side for many years past. We have to go back to* Valkyrie II *to find a midship section that bears any similarity to the easy bilges and full garboards that distinguish* Shamrock III *so sharply from any of her immediate predecessors, and in this respect, she is the most "wholesome" yacht of any of the existing challengers and defenders of the 90-foot class. Having said this much, it has to be admitted that all the other characteristic features of the boat are marked by the extremes of beam, draft, and overall length to which designers have been driven in their attempt to carry a maximum amount of sail under a rule which, unfortunately, puts no limit whatever upon sail area—an unfortunate omission, to which more than anything else is to be attributed the absurdly exaggerated proportions of the modern racing 90-footer. Although her midship section is large, the lines, which have been carried out with the skill that characterizes all the Fife boats, are so sweet and fair that she looks at first glance more like a 70-footer than a boat built up to the full 90-foot limit.*

All period reports indicate that with her exaggerated proportions, the *Reliance* had a strong family likeness to earlier Herreshoff boats. In drawing out her lines to such an extreme length, Herreshoff produced an extremely handsome craft. The hard turn of the midship sections at the bilges is softened out gradually as the forward and after ends of the waterline are reached, with the result that the overhangs themselves are very symmetrical and show a sweetness of modeling that goes far to redeem their disproportional length. The deck line does not flow toward the bow and stern with so flat a curve as had been customary in earlier Herreshoff boats, with the result that when she heels, she will take a very long bearing, and there will be no hard spot or shoulder to pile up the water when driven at high speed.

One of the most striking features in the boat is the long, drawn-out bow projecting nearly thirty feet beyond the waterline. The *Scientific American* writer echoed the concerns of many seasoned yachtsmen who wondered why the bow was not made shorter relative to the stern, reasoning that every foot of length can be utilized. No greater authority than Herreshoff regarded the *Reliance* as something of an experiment; he said that only the actual test in a jump of sea off Newport or Sandy Hook could determine the value of such an extreme bow.

The following is an excerpt from Nat Herreshoff's 1934 recollection of the *Reliance*:[7]

*In the fall of 1902, there was another challenge for the America's Cup and the order was given us about [the] first of November. We had already taken [an] order for an eighty-six feet waterline schooner [Ingomar], and the class of Bar Harbor thirty-One Footers (11), and others besides the usual number of steamers. So, our shops were quite full. Mr. Iselin had recovered his health and again became manager of a new Cup defender, this the fourth time. She was owned by a syndicate of very distinguished yachtsmen of the New York Yacht Club. She became to be named* Reliance *and to carry out Mr. Iselin's wishes, she favored too much of the scow type, above the water, to be a good type of big yacht. She was very powerful, having about one hundred eight and one-half tons of lead low down. She was one hundred and forty-three feet overall, ninety feet waterline, twenty-five feet nine inches beam, with bronze plating over a steel frame of my longitudinal plan of construction, and very strong for its weight, though hardly equal to the pounding due to [the] scow form of bow. Her rig was enormous [with a] boom [of] one hundred and fifteen feet four inches by twenty-four inches diameter, [a] gaff [of] seventy-two feet, [a] #1 club topsail yard [of] sixty-eight feet, [a] spinnaker boom [of] eighty-three feet four inches and others in proportion. The #1 club topsail reached one hundred eighty-nine feet six inches above water and bowsprit end to boom end was two hundred*

Captain Nat's Noble Trio: the *Constitution* (left), the *Columbia* (center) and the *Reliance*.

*and two feet eight inches. All the major spars were steel. Her mainsails were probably the largest ever made and were of 000 and 0000 duck. He* [Mr. Iselin] *made four, I think, all of specially woven duck for the purpose. Her crew was sixty-eight all told, and Charles Barr was captain. With the exception of the main boom being lengthened two and one-half feet and* [the] *gaff two feet, so she would balance well with* [a] *larger sized jib topsail, there was no change made on her and she never had any accidents to require new parts or changes except reinforcing the plating under the bow two or three times. Both* Constitution *and* Columbia *were fitted out for trial craft and* [with the *Reliance*] *they made a noble trio.*

[The] Reliance *proved always faster to windward and before the wind, but not any faster in reaching, and in fact, not as fast as* [the] Constitution. *This could not be explained, for due to a much longer bilge line and longer useful length due to extreme overhangs, it was expected this would be her best point of sailing. These trials demonstrated* Constitution *to be faster than* Columbia *as was indicated in their early meetings.*

*I sailed in most of* Reliance's *races and often took the helm, so* [Charles] *Barr could check up the trim of sails or rest. She easily defended the Cup against* Shamrock III. *It is interesting that in the first unfinished race, started in a light north westerly and quite a ground swell, in going fifteen miles to leeward with spinnakers and pounding into the seas, we ran away from* Shamrock *between two and three miles.* [The] *race was called off in calm.*

The *Reliance* and the *Shamrock III* eventually met in late August; the *Reliance* won the first meet by seven minutes, due largely to bad sail handling by the British boat's crew. The *Reliance* won the second race by one minute, nineteen seconds, corrected time. Then, because of a lack of wind, the third race was delayed for nine days, with a one-day delay for fear of the yachts being demasted because of near-gale-force winds.

The 1903 series finished on September 3 in foggy weather. The race came to its awkward finish when *Shamrock III* became lost in the fog, totally missing the mark and winding up northeast of the lightship.

## SHAMROCK IV

After the 1903 match, no challenges came over until 1907, when Lipton issued a conditional challenge. His condition was for a new measurement

rule, which would take into account displacement as well as length and sail area. The new criterion for craft measurement, called the Universal Rule calculated by Nathanael G. Herreshoff, is discussed in chapter seven.

After negotiating with the New York Yacht Club in 1912, when both sides agreed to favor smaller and less expensive yachts than had previously raced,

The *Resolute*, with Charles Francis Adams at the helm, marked the first Cup race in which amateur skippers commanded and the last series sailed in New York waters.

Lipton challenged with his *Shamrock IV*, a 75-foot boat carrying 10,495 feet of sail. She was on her way over to the scene of the match when the European war began, resulting in the contest's cancellation. It did not occur again until 1920.

The *Shamrock IV*, designed by Charles E. Nicholson, was not a very handsome craft, and even Nicholson referred to her as the "ugly duckling." Nicholson, the designer of several successful English yachts, had not yet designed a yacht to the specifications of the Universal Rule. Before building regulations became part of the measurement requirements, Nicholson endeavored to build an extremely light hull with a great deal of laminated wood.

The pleasing-to-the-eye lines of the *Shamrock IV* are pictured on this circa 1920 photo postcard.

L. Francis Herreshoff, in his *An Introduction to Yachting*, writes his opinion on the *Shamrock IV*:

> *Above water, she was quite scow-shaped so that her lines were adapted to high speed, but below water, her lines were as full as other Universal Rule boats, otherwise she would have rated very high. Although she had a very high measurement rating for her waterline length of 75 feet, her final rating was over 94 feet, but many Universal Rule boats of that time rated nearly the same as their waterline length and later ones rated considerably less than their waterline length.*

The three yachts built for the defense included: the *Resolute*, a Herreshoff creation for a New York Yacht Club syndicate; the *Defiance*, designed by

George Owen for Boston, New York and Philadelphia yachtsmen; and the *Vanitie*, by William Gardner, for Alexander S. Cochran, all just under a seventy-five-foot waterline.

Captain Nat Herreshoff had much experience building Cup defenders, while Owen, Gardner and Nicholson had never previously designed a boat to challenge for the Cup, nor did they have the benefit as Herreshoff did of having use of his own construction company.

Again, we reference L. Francis Herreshoff for his opinion of the defender candidates:

> [The] Defiance *was of composite construction with mahogany planking and though her hull was considered a good design both in model and construction, her sail plan was probably her weakest point for she had her mast stepped well forward with a very small fore triangle…this arrangement allows only small balloon jib and spinnaker. Her other great trouble was that she was built by six or seven* [boat building] *concerns.*
>
> [The] Vanitie *had two or three disadvantages, the first was that she rated rather high; second, her actual freeboard was too low but she had bulwarks along her top sides, which carried considerable weight of water on deck at times. Her third defect was that she had none of the mechanical devices for handling sheets and backstays, which had been developed for the last three Cup boats.*
>
> *In* Resolute, *Mr. Herreshoff made the diplomatic mistake of designing* [the boat] *to rate quite low which…was a great handicap to her. The reason he did this was that there had been much talk about the expense of Cup boats since the previous races in 1903 between the gigantic* Reliance *and* Shamrock III, *and he thought the best way to reduce cost was to design a small, low rating yacht.*
>
> [The] Resolute *as she came out was a nicely proportioned yacht with small sail area, but while the boat-to-boat finishes between her and* Vanitie *were often close,* Resolute, *as originally rigged, beat* Vanitie *quite easily with time allowance.*

Listed below are the scores of the three defense contenders at the end of the first season of trials:

| | |
|---|---|
| *Resolute* | 15 firsts out of 18 starts |
| *Vanitie* | 5 firsts out of 20 starts |
| *Defiance* | 0 firsts out of 10 starts |

For the 1915 series of defender trials, the *Resolute* afterguard convinced Mr. Herreshoff to give her more sail in order to increase her rating. Listed below are the scores at the end of the second season of trials:

| | |
|---|---|
| *Resolute* | 12 firsts out of 16 starts |
| *Vanitie* | 4 firsts out of 16 starts |

The *Defiance* withdrew after the 1914 trials. The *Resolute* was selected after a lively series with the *Vanitie* off Newport, Rhode Island.

# First Race

The first of the final races in which the boat that won three out of five matches took the Cup was on July 15 with amateur helmsmen Sir William P. Burton, skipper of the *Shamrock IV*, and Charles F. Adams, skipper of the *Resolute*.

We now return to L. Francis Herreshoff's succinct description of the conditions and outcome of the five matches:

> *They started at noontime in a very light, fluky southerly breeze to sail over windward and leeward course of thirty miles. At the time, a thunderstorm was making up over the Jersey shore and the sky was very dark toward the southwest almost in the direction the yachts were sailing. Both of the yachts seemed to foot at about the same speed but* Resolute *pointed perceptibly higher. Some people said she was sheeted too flat for the light weather. However, in a half hour or so the defender was said to be a quarter mile to windward of the challenger. The wind then became very light but* Resolute *seemed to carry her way very well and worked up to a lead of perhaps half a mile. Then the thunderstorm struck with a heavy deluge of rain and resounding thunder but not much wind. After the rainsquall, a light breeze came from the southwest and the challenger took a tack close under the Jersey shore and stood in so far that she had to pay off to clear the buoy off Shrewsbury Rocks.*
>
> *…*Resolute *was pointing high enough to make the mark with a lead of perhaps half a mile. During this time,* Shamrock IV *had tacked ship several times and once or twice* Resolute *tacked to keep between the mark and her adversary, but she was too far ahead to affect the challenger's wind. As they were nearing the weather mark,* Resolute's *mainsail began to sag at the throat and finally the forward end of the gaff came almost all the*

*way down. She continued for a while under her headsails and the triangular after part of her mainsail, rounding the weather mark some four and a half minutes ahead of the challenger, then dropped out of the race and headed for her anchorage under her jib.*

## SECOND RACE

*On July 20,* Shamrock IV *sailed a remarkable race. Soon after the start, the challenger had trouble in setting her balloon jib and finally tore it. In its place, some sort of a reaching jib was set from her topmast at a point higher up than her working jib was set, and with this sail under her jib topsail, she went very fast. She laid a course quite a little to weather of where* Resolute *was sailing with her regular balloon jib set, and sailed by the defender.*

*At the first mark, the challenger had a lead of four minutes, thirty-two seconds. It was a close reach to the next mark in light to moderate breeze, and this was about the only condition under which the challenger was fast, and she opened up her lead, it is said to nearly a mile. The wind then changed to more ahead and freshened and the challenger, which had a good lead, got it about five minutes before the defender and romped toward the finish line to beat* Resolute *boat-to-boat ten minutes and five seconds. After subtraction of the seven minutes thirty-nine seconds the challenger allowed the defender, she had beaten her [by] two minutes and twenty-six seconds, thus making the challenger two up.*

## THIRD RACE

*Although the challenger got the start by nineteen seconds and footed faster than* Resolute, *the defender pointed higher and made less leeway so she was soon to windward of* Shamrock IV *who tacked many times in an effort to get her wind free, but* Resolute, *with her fast working sheet and backstay winches, seemed to get her sails trimmed so much faster that she gained perceptibly when both yachts tacked.*

*It is said that* Shamrock IV *came about eighteen times in the beat to windward. When they rounded,* Resolute *had a lead of one minute and forty-seven seconds. On the way home the wind increased so that running under spinnaker the challenger passed the defender near the finish line making* [this finish] *next to the closest finish boat-to-boat of the Cup races.* Resolute *with her big handicap, won quite easily making the score now one to two in favor of the challenger.*

# FOURTH RACE

*Both yachts tried hard to get the start in this important race and Sir William succeeded in taking the challenger over with a lead of twenty-three seconds. When they reached the windward or first mark the wind was ten or more knots and as* Resolute *only had a lead of two minutes and ten seconds the spectators thought it was not enough to keep her ahead on the next two legs of the course, which were reaches and expected to favor the challenger. There was a strong breeze by that time and both yachts covered this ten-mile leg of the course at a rate of twelve knots or more, but* Shamrock IV *only gained a little on the defender for at the second mark the defender had a lead of one minute and twenty-seven seconds.*

*On the last leg there was a squall making up and as it approached,* Shamrock IV *took in both her topsail and jib topsail while* Resolute *seemed to think she could luff through it with only her jib topsail down. In this fluky air the challenger caught up to and apparently got ahead of the defender, but the wind swung back to the south whereupon* Resolute *set a ballooner and tacked to leeward and thus picked up a breeze, or as the sailor would say, "made her own wind," going at a good rate toward the finish line which she crossed three minutes and fourteen seconds ahead of* Shamrock IV. *The yachts were now both two up.*

# FIFTH RACE

*The last race of July 27 was in very light weather and someone had persuaded* [Mr. Herreshoff] *the designer of* Resolute *to sail on her although he was seventy-two years old. This race was a windward and leeward on in which the start was postponed...for lack of wind. The starting line was in a calm streak with a light northwest wind inshore... Both yachts held back for the two-minute handicap gun and crossed the line at two-seventeen* [p.m.]. *The challenger seemed to slip along quite as well as the defender, but the latter somehow appeared to be working windward of her so that after a while, with their cross tacking,* [Charles Francis] *Adams brought* Resolute *about almost dead to windward of the challenger.*

The result of these exciting races was Sir Tom's fourth loss to the Cup defender, 3–2.

## SHAMROCK V

Sir Tom built the *Shamrock V* in 1930 for his fifth and last attempt to wrench the America's Cup from the halls of the New York Yacht Club. This challenger was the first British yacht built to the new J-class Rule and the last of the Js built entirely of wood. After launch, she was continually upgraded with changes to her hull and rudder. Her rig was modified to create the most efficient racing sail plan; but alas, she was no match for the faster *Enterprise*.

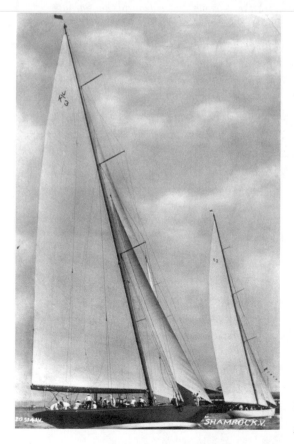

In this dramatic image, Lipton's *Shamrock V* is seen trailing Vanderbilt's *Enterprise. A period real photo postcard by Valentine's Publishing*

The *Enterprise* crew is captured in this September 2, 1930 photo sharpening their tactics a few days before the scheduled Cup races.

Sportswriters' reports about the 1930 Cup races express almost universal agreement that they were far less exciting than the trials. Edwin P. Hoyt, in his 1969 book, *The Defenders*, quotes one reporter as describing the first race as "the dullest race sailed in American waters [Narragansett Bay] all year."

*Above*: In this 1930 camera study, Lipton's contender for the America's Cup, the *Shamrock V* (foreground), is racing in her shakedown trials with the *Cambria* (left) and the *Candida* (right).

*Below*: The *Enterprise* exits Herreshoff's construction shed with celebratory flags flying.

Hoyt continues:

*Captain Vanderbilt took* Enterprise *out in front at the start and led all the way, finishing 2 minutes and 52 seconds ahead.* Enterprise *won the second race by more than 9 minutes.* Shamrock V *made a better start in the third race, and managed to blanket* Enterprise *for a few minutes, but Vanderbilt tacked away from his opponent, cleared his wind, and began to edge ahead. Then* Shamrock's *main halyard gave away, and the mainsail sagged. The race was over,* Shamrock *having to default. The fourth race was sailed in the best wind of the series at 14 knots over a triangular course. The crew of* Enterprise *noticed a change in the wind before the* Shamrock *and got off to a fine start, increasing the lead until at the halfway mark the defender was 9 minutes and 10 seconds ahead. She loafed home, letting* Shamrock V *catch up a bit, and still won the race by 5 minutes and 44 seconds, to finish the series of 1930.*

The British twelve-meter yacht the *Lionheart* (left) and the *France 3* pull apart after colliding just prior to the start of their semifinal challenger series off Newport on August 26, 1980. *UPI wire photo.*

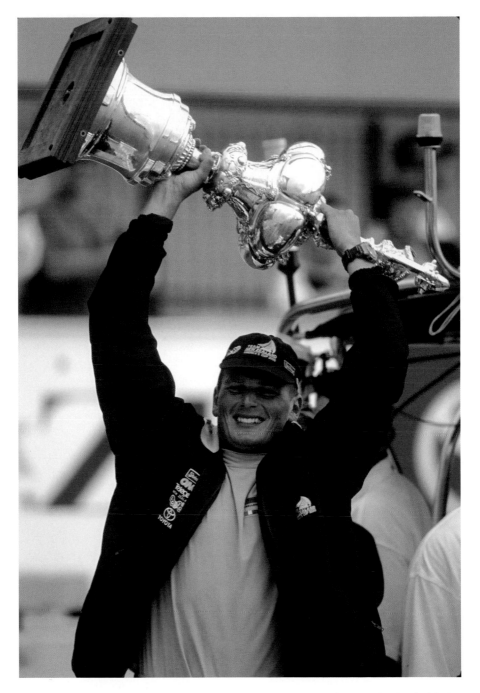

Dean Barker triumphantly hoists the coveted Cup over his head after New Zealand's *Black Magic* wins a sweeping 5–0 victory over *Stars & Stripes* in the 1995 match in San Diego. *Onne van der Wal. Vanderwal.com.*

*Stars & Stripes* is the name of a series of the America's Cup yachts skippered by Dennis Conner. The name "Stars & Stripes" refers to the expression of endearment often used for the flag of the United States. *Onne van der Wal. Vanderwal.com.*

Conner's 1995 yacht, the *Stars & Stripes* (USA-34), won the defender series, the Citizen Cup against the *Young America* (USA-36) and the "Mighty Mary" (USA-43), by use of superior tactics. However, it was considered the slowest of the three defending yachts, partially due to an inventory of old sails. *Onne van der Wal. Vanderwal.com.*

*Above*: The Twenty-ninth America's Cup was contested between the winner of the 1995 Citizen Cup, team Dennis Conner, with the *Stars & Stripes* (ex–*Young America*, USA 36), and the winner of the 1995 Louis Vuitton Cup, team New Zealand, with the *Black Magic* (NZL 32). *Onne van der Wal. Vanderwal.com.*

*Left*: In this photo, the *Young America*, with her name changed to *Stars & Stripes*, battles the aggressive *Black Magic* (NZL 32) for a commanding position. Team Dennis Conner selected to use the *Young America*, considered the faster defender, instead of *Stars & Stripes* in the America's Cup final, losing to team New Zealand. *Onne van der Wal. Vanderwal.com.*

Team New Zealand, representing the Royal New Zealand Yacht Squadron, is the pride of its home country following consecutive wins in the America's Cup matches in 1995 and 2000. In doing this, it became the first team from a country outside the United States to successfully win and then defend the America's Cup. *Onne van der Wal. Vanderwal.com.*

The Kiwis' success in the America's Cup competitions has contributed to New Zealand's reputation for producing excellent sailors and boat designers. The 1995 challenge had everything—the boat *Black Magic* was fast, it had a smart crew led by skipper Russell Coutts and Sir Peter Blake ably backed the team. *Onne van der Wal. Vanderwal.com.*

Team New Zealand's *Black Magic* (NZL 60) successfully defended the Cup against Italy's Prada Challenge winner, the *Luna Rossa* (ITA 45), 5–0, in the 2000 Cup Defense. *Onne van der Wal. Vanderwal.com.*

A strong two-boat challenge sponsored by Prada, the team formed in 1997. The team used designer German Frers, who worked for *Il Moro di Venezia* in 1992. Francesco de Angelis was the skipper, with Rod Davis acting as the sailing coach. *Onne van der Wal. Vanderwal.com.*

Prada originally acquired two boats from the America syndicate before building ITA 45 and ITA 48. *Onne van der Wal. Vanderwal.com.*

The America's Cup. *Onne van der Wal. Vanderwal.com.*

Like a well-oiled machine, the *Stars & Stripes*' crew attends to its many tasks, giving the craft an edge in speed and tactics. *Onne van der Wal. Vanderwal.com.*

# Chapter 7

# NEW RULES,
# NEW CHALLENGERS

## THE UNIVERSAL RULE

From 1920 to 1937, the Universal Rule determined a yacht's eligibility to enter America's Cup races. Yachts built according to the rule reached their peak in the super J-class yachts. Before 1920, the Seawanhaka Rule was used, and after 1937, smaller boats were desirable, so the Universal Rule regained its popularity and became the standard.

Yacht designer Nathanael Greene Herreshoff devised the rule in 1903. Up until that time, Herreshoff had designed winning Cup defenders that fully exploited the Seawanhaka Rule. This rule was based on only a yacht's waterline length and sail area, thus creating narrow boats with long overhangs. This reached its peak with the defender of the 1903 America's Cup, the *Reliance*, which many sportswriters described as a "racing freak," and prompted Herreshoff to propose a rule that also took into account the displacement of the boat.

For years, a growing dissatisfaction existed among yachtsmen over the type of boat developed under the measurement rules governing yacht racing. The complaint was that the construction of yachts pushed lightness to such an extreme that broken spars and leaking hulls were increasingly common. Many owners complained that the form of the yachts had gone to such extreme proportions that such racers were exceedingly costly to build, troublesome to handle and subject to rapid deterioration. Some designers espoused the thought that such construction and modeling combined to

The *Reliance*, built under the Universal Rule, was the most spectacular yacht in the long tradition of the America's Cup, being far larger than all previous challengers and defenders.

render these boats about the very worst kind of seagoing craft that can be designed. As cruisers, they are preeminently uncomfortable and unsafe. The question was to develop a rule of measurement under which it is possible to produce a yacht that is both speedy and comfortable—one that, when its racing days are over, will still have before it a long life of usefulness as a cruiser.

In 1902, the New York Yacht Club appointed a committee on measurement that would "produce a wholesome type of boat" and ask whether designers considered it possible to "formulate a system of measurement which might be adopted as an international standard." The committee requested that suggestions be sent in detailing what system of measurement should be adopted. The replies received were unanimous in agreeing that it was practicable to formulate the desired rule and that displacement or its equivalent should be incorporated as a factor in the rule of measurement adopted. Because of the discussion thus opened, it developed that there was a practical agreement on the three elements of length, sail area and displacement as those that should enter into the question of measurement.

The rule finally adopted by the New York Yacht Club is the length multiplied by the square root of the sail area and divided by five times the cubed root of the displacement; thus, the Universal Rule became the standard measurement rule.

In the new rule, length is no longer measured on the middle vertical plane of the vessel but on a vertical longitudinal plane taken at one-quarter of the greatest beam at the load waterline. It is obtained by measuring the length in the plane at the waterline and on deck, adding these together and dividing by two, which gives the mean length on the quarter breadth.

It is worthy to note the effect that the new rule has on existing yachts: for example, the *Columbia*, whose rating under the old rule was 102, becomes 131 under the new rule.

# INTERNATIONAL RULE

Shortly after acceptance of the Universal Rule, an international conference convened in Europe to develop a better rating rule. The objective of the meeting was to make improvements to the Universal Rule; instead, a new rule was developed, which actually accomplished the same purposes but in different ways. This new rule, written and agreed upon, became the so-called International Rule, and that memorable accomplishment occurred in 1907.

The July 27, 1920 start of the fifth race in the 1920 Cup defense. The *Shamrock IV* is leading the *Resolute*. Skipper Charles Francis Adams saved the Cup by working the *Resolute* into the lead in this race and won by the largest margin in forty years.

Interestingly, the two rules gave birth to roughly similar boats. Both rules produced long, narrow, deep boats, although weighty by twenty-first-century standards. These boats are speedy upwind, but because of their required high displacement, they are not as speedy downwind as their modern cousins.

For almost twenty-five years, until 1931, the dual rules produced fine racing boats. However, there was one vexing problem: when an owner of a Universal Rule boat endeavored to race in Europe, it became necessary to build a new boat according to the International Rule The same problem existed for the European wishing to race in America. Because the rating rules produced somewhat different boats, it became impossible to race boats built according to the different rules without time handicaps.

To solve this problem, a New York Yacht Club committee met in 1931 with representatives from Europe. The agreement reached stated that, forthwith, all large boats would adhere to the Universal Rule and small boats to the International Rule. This decision made sense since the Universal Rule clearly seemed to produce better large boats, and the International Rule seemed to produce better small boats.

# TWELVE-METER RULE

World War II interrupted the Cup race; after the war, there was scant interest in financing a new challenge. The New York Yacht Club reasoned that, for consideration of syndicate sponsorship, the challenge and defense teams should sail in smaller boats, and it was time to change the rules again.

Twelve-meter yachts are big, and they are expensive, but they are only half the overall length and carry an eighth of the sail area of some of the yachts that sailed in Cup races in the early decades of the twentieth century.

The New York Supreme Court ruled in 1956 that boats in the America's Cup match races should be in

The twelve-meter sloop *Nefertiti* under sail for the first time off Marblehead, Massachusetts. The billowing spinnaker was borrowed from the schooner *Lord Jim*, owned by E. Ross Anderson, the leading backer of the $300,000 yacht. *AP wire photo, May 28, 1962.*

the twelve-meter class. The court also ruled that there is no need for the boats to travel by sail to the place of competition. This ruling allows boats to be ferried to the site of the competition on cargo ships or flown aboard large-capacity cargo airplanes.

This is how a twelve-meter is calculated: "L" stands for length but is not a matter of measuring the boat from stem to stern; "d" is for the boat's area; and "2" is displacement. "Sa" is the sail area, although in reality, the entire mainsail is measured but only 85 percent of the foresail. "F" is the average amount of freeboard—that is, the distance from the waterline to the edge of the deck when the boat is lying vertically. Measure in three places just to be certain that 2.37 is truthfully 2.37, and the answer should always be 12.00.

The result cannot be greater than 12.00 meters or 39.37 feet.

The formula, equated to a balloon, compresses in one part and gets bigger in another part. If you desire a long waterline, your sail will be smaller. If you want to carry a lot of sail, you must shorten the waterline.

When all the measurements are double-checked and added, the sum should be twelve, or perhaps less, but certainly never more.

The first summer of racing in international twelve-meter-class yachts was in 1958, when all the twelves raced in July in the New York Yacht Club's annual cruise.

# THE IACC RULE

Since the International America's Cup Class (IACC) Rule was established for the 1992 Cup races, it has been regulating the design and construction of America's Cup racing yachts. There are limits placed on the main speed-producing factors of sail area, length, draft and displacement.

Version 5.0 of the IACC Rule came about on December 15, 2003. The amended rule allows a greater downwind sail area and a deeper keel, with a reduction of overall weight by one ton. This change produces faster and livelier yachts.

Typical parameters of an IACC yacht are:

Length: 75 feet
Weight: 37,000 tons
Height of the mast: 119 feet
Spinnaker: 4,500 square feet
Main and jib: 3,000 square feet
Crew: 17 members

## Chapter 8

# THE J-BOATS ARE
# A' COMING

After Lipton's fourth defeat, nearly a decade passed before the New York Yacht Club received another challenge. An important agreement reached in 1930 by all seafaring nations with a potential interest in challenging for the Cup made significant changes in marine architecture and rating of yachts, and the introduction of multiple classes of yachts was established.

Sir Tom's last attempt to win the Old Mug signaled the end of an epoch as far as boat design is concerned. The *Shamrock V* is exactly like the 1930 defender, the J-boat *Enterpris*.

J-boats are long, beautiful sloops between 120 and 135 feet in overall length, with a waterline of at least 65 feet. These are smaller than previous Cup racers. The reason for this is that if size is reduced, more boats can participate. If more take part, there is a better chance of getting better challengers.

The America's Cup competition adopted the J-class in 1928, considering the next regatta in 1930. The class itself, though, dates back to the turn of the century at the time of international acceptance of the Universal Rule. J-class yachts were the largest constructed under the Universal Rule. There were only ten J-class yachts designed and built. Additionally, several yachts of closely related dimensions, mostly twenty-three-meter International Rule boats, converted to J-class after their construction to meet the rating rules.

Further refinements were made in the measurements of the yachts, and the J-class sloop of seventy-six-foot rating became the rule. This signaled the advent of the Marconi rig, one that omitted gaffs, topsails and overhanging booms. Since the design of both yachts is to the same rating formula, time allowances are no longer necessary.

The following is an example of the new class rating: a boat of seventy-six feet fell into the J-class, and a sixty-five-foot boat fell into the K-class. However, there are variances in the rating system for the designer. As long as certain specifications are included in the yacht's design, a J-boat is allowed a waterline length of eighty-seven feet, thus putting boats with shorter waterline length but stronger in other design principles on an even keel with the larger boats. The rule actually includes provisions for an even larger type of boat, the I-class, though none was built. Inquiries made in the 1930s for a defense in the smaller K-class were rejected.

However, J-boat construction only lasted from 1930 to 1937, with three challenges in that period. The 1934 match was the most difficult for the Cup defender. The challenger, the flying ace and airplane manufacturer Sir Thomas O.M. Sopwith, came over with his J-boat, the *Endeavour*. The defender, Harold S. Vanderbilt, skippered his boat, the *Rainbow*. It soon became abundantly clear that the challenger was the faster boat, and Sopwith won the first two matches easily.

For the third and following three matches, Vanderbilt handed the wheel over to Sherman Hoyt. Continued good luck and cool nerves allowed the *Rainbow* to win all four races, and the Cup remained in the possession of the New York Yacht Club

The J-class yachts were the first to race in an America's Cup match governed by a formal design rule. Minimum and maximum lengths set forth in the Deed of Gift restricted only previous defenders and challengers. Sir Thomas Lipton, challenging in 1930 for the fifth time, had held earlier discussions with the New York Yacht Club in the hopes of adopting the Universal Rule for the previous America's Cup match, intended for 1914 but delayed until 1920. Though an agreement to use the rule did not come to fruition for that match, the 1914 boats *Vanitie* and *Resolute* still roughly followed J-class parameters.

# THE *ENTERPRISE*, LAUNCHED APRIL 14, 1930

The 1930 Cup defender, the *Enterprise*, designed by W. Starling Burgess and built by the Herreshoff Manufacturing Company, was the first to use the so-called Park Avenue boom. A circular-sectioned double-skin duralumin mast built by the Geleen L. Martin Company replaced the original spruce

The Aldrich-Vanderbilt Cup defender, the *Enterprise*.

mast. Other innovations included Tobin bronze plating; a triple-headed rig, trialed with retracting spreaders; a waterline length of 80 feet; and an overall length of 120 feet. The *Enterprise* was adversely affected by rule changes for 1934 requiring full accommodations for crew and placing winches above deck. The Aldrich syndicate—Harold Vanderbilt, Vincent Astor, George Baker, George Whitney, Floyd Carlisle and E. Walter Clarke—financed the *Enterprise*. She was broken up in September 1935 at the Herreshoff boatyard.

# THE *WHIRLWIND*, LAUNCHED MAY 7, 1930

The Thorne-Hammond syndicate
Cup defender, the *Whirlwind*.

The Boston firm George Lawley & Son built the *Whirlwind* designed by L. Francis Herreshoff for the Landon Thorne syndicate. This double-ended craft, inspired by Nat Herreshoff's M-class *Istalena*, sported mahogany planking and a pine deck over steel frames; a waterline length of 80 feet; and an overall length of 130 feet. A duralumin mast replaced the original spruce mast. She was the first "J" with a double-headsail rig and electric wind-speed indicators. The Whirlwind syndicate members included Landon Thorne, Alfred Loomis and Paul Hammond. They scrapped the yacht in 1935 at City Island.

## *SHAMROCK V*, THE 1930 CHALLENGER

The Camper & Nicholson yard in Gosport built the *Shamrock V*, designed by Charles Nicholson. Sturdy and well built, her skin was mahogany planking over steel frames, with a yellow pine deck; teak stem, sternposts and counter-timbers; a hollow spruce mast, elliptical section; and a lower sail area but greater rig height relative to other Js. Her waterline length was 81.1 feet, and her overall length was 119.8, with a displacement of 134 tons. She was extensively tuned up in the Solent, racing against the *Shamrock IV* before the 1930 challenge.

After Lipton's final loss, he sold the *Shamrock V* to Thomas O.M. Sopwith in 1932. Sopwith modified the yacht's hull and rudder; he later sold her to Sir Richard Fairey, who after the war sold her to Mario Crespi. Crespi sold her to Piero Scanu in 1962, and Scanu renamed her *Quattrofoglio* (spelling uncertain but roughly "Four Leaf" in Italian as a play on her original name). By this time, she may have become ketch rigged. She was rebuilt at Camper & Nicholson in 1967–70 and sold to the Lipton Tea Company in 1986. The tea company later donated her to the Newport (Rhode Island) Museum of Yachting. In 1989, Elizabeth Meyer restored the rig, bulwarks and deckhouse to original specifications and in 1995 sold her to the Newport Yacht Restoration School, which in turn sold her to the Newport *Shamrock V* Corporation in 1998. She underwent another refitting in 2000 at Pendennis, under Gerard Dykstra, who sold her to Marcos de Maraes of Brazil. Maraes sails her today as a pleasure yacht.

# The *Yankee*, Launched May 10, 1930

The *Yankee*, designed by Frank Paine, son of General Charles J. Paine, consigned construction of the yacht to George Lawley & Son. The *Yankee* syndicate included John Lawrence, Charles Francis Adams and Chandler Hovey. Her specifications were: a mast of spruce, Tobin bronze plating and a triple-headed rig, a waterline length of 84 feet and an overall length of 126 feet. The *Yankee* took part in the 1930 defense trials, but she was swamped by the *Enterprise*. In 1934, the *Yankee*, with a modified bow, slightly longer waterline and increased sail area, joined the defender trials, nearly beating out the *Rainbow*, the eventual 1934 defender.

With Gerard Lambert as the *Yankee*'s new owner, her racing days continued. In 1935, she sailed to England, racing Lambert's schooner the *Atlantic* and winning the cross-ocean contest by seventeen hours. She spent the season racing in England, taking eight first-place finishes in thirty-two races.

Buoyed by her successes in English waters, in 1937 she again entered the defender trials, this time testing a single-headed rig, a mast step moved forward, a lowered center of ballast and a larger mainsail. Again unsuccessful in obtaining the defender's mantle, Lambert sold the yacht as scrap in April 1941.

## THE *WEETAMOE*, LAUNCHED MAY 10, 1930

The Nichols-Morgan syndicate Cup defender, the *Weetamoe*.

The *Weetamoe* syndicate, consisting of George Nichols, J.P. Morgan, Cornelius Vanderbilt, Arthur Curtiss James, George T. Bowdoin, Henry Walters and Gerard Lambert, hired Clinton Crane to design its yacht, which was built by the Herreshoff Manufacturing Company. The yacht, built with Tobin bronze plating with a triple-headed rig, had a waterline length of 83 feet and an overall length of 125.5 feet. In October 1930, the syndicate sold the *Weetamoe* to Fredrick Henry Prince, who intended to enter her in the 1934 defender trials. Prince modified her hull and added a larger and heavier keel, which resulted in a slower craft; she was later restored to her original configuration. The *Weetamoe* raced in the off years between Cup defenses.

## THE *RAINBOW*, LAUNCHED MAY 15, 1934

The *Rainbow* syndicate included some of the most prestigious names in American industry and finance, notably Harold S., Alfred G., Frederick W. and William K. Vanderbilt. The *Rainbow*, designed by W. Starling Burgess, is the last Herreshoff-built America's Cup yacht. With a waterline length of 82 feet and an overall length of 126.7 feet, she sported a duralumin mast built by the Glenn L. Martin Company and an innovative bending boom and bar rigging. She successfully defended the Cup in the 1934 match. She was scrapped in Fall River, Massachusetts, in August 1940.

The *Rainbow*, a J-class yacht designed by W. Starling Burgess and financed and sailed by Harold Vanderbilt. Yachting *magazine,* September 1934.

# THE *RANGER*, LAUNCHED MAY 11, 1937

W. Starling Burgess and Olin Stephens II designed the *Ranger* schematic from models tested in the Stevens Institute towing tank (see *America's Cup Trials and Triumphs,* 2010). The final yacht shape has elements of both men's ideas. Innovative concepts include a flush riveted steel hull, heat-treated steel rod shrouds and translucent Bakelite deck inserts. At a cost of $500,000, the keel was laid down in December 1936. Launched from Bath Iron Works as Hull No. 172, the *Ranger,* fully funded by Vanderbilt, was the largest displacement J-class Cup defender built. She lost her mast on a delivery cruise off Cape Cod, later replaced with a used wheel, rigging and sails salvaged from the *Rainbow* and the *Enterprise.* She was hauled at the end of 1937 and sold for scrap in May 1941.

We learn the following about this "Super J" from the 2001 *Herreshoff Marine Museum Chronicle*:

> *The only new rig gimmicks of* Ranger *were a Duralumin mast and bar steel rigging. She used many sails from older boats, and even her designers*

W. Starling Burgess and Olin Stephens II co-designed the *Ranger*. She was the first of the modern racing yachts to cost $500,000.

*reduced their fees. In 1937 [during the Great Depression], it was good just to be working.*

*She was launched May 11 and set out amid a noisy serenade of whistles and cheers, towing to Newport astern of Vanderbilt's motor yacht Vara. It was a brave sight as the big white sloop swept out of the Kennebec into the Gulf of Maine, her tall new mast towering above the rocks and pines of the coastline, but she was an incredibly sorry spectacle the following morning when she ended up in Marblehead minus the fancy new stick, her rigging a cat's cradle of snarled metal on her deck. Somehow, some of her upper rigging carried away early in the night as she rolled her way south over large swells, and the result was a progression of disaster.*

## THE *ENDEAVOUR*, THE 1934 CHALLENGER

Owner Thomas O.M. Sopwith contracted Charles Nicholson to design his new Cup challenger using aeronautical technology at the Camper & Nicholson yard and a steel hull and mast, and a Park Avenue boom later replaced her original "North Circular" bending boom. The *Endeavour* is the first yacht to use the double-clewed quadrilateral jib.

After a mid-ocean mishap while returning to England in 1937, she was laid up at the Camper & Nicholson yard until 1947, when she was sold as

For the fifteenth running for the America's Cup, Charles E. Nicholson designed and Camper & Nicholson built the J-class sloop *Endeavour* for Thomas O.M. Sopwith. Yachting *magazine, September 1934.*

scrap. The salvage of lead from her keel never took place, and she sat as an abandoned hulk until purchased by the British Maritime Trust in 1973 for £10. John Amos began her restoration in 1983. In 1984, Amos sold the partly restored yacht to Elizabeth Meyer, who completed the restoration. Beginning in 1989, the rehabilitated *Endeavour* sailed as a charter boat in Narragansett Bay for the next fifteen years. Cassio Antunes purchased the *Endeavour* in 2006 for a reported $13.1 million; he announced his plan to base the seventy-two-year-old J-boat in the Cayman Islands and Cascais, Portugal, and to restore the British red ensign.

## *ENDEAVOUR II*, LAUNCHED JUNE 8, 1936

Thomas O.M. Sopwith again contracted Charles Nicholson to design his new Cup challenger, the *Endeavour II*, for the 1937 races. This yacht featured a well-built flush-plated steel hull; a steel centerboard; steel framing, planking

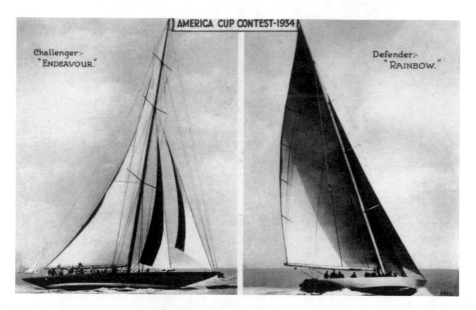

The 1934 challenger for the coveted Cup, the sloop *Endeavour* (left), was skippered by owner Thomas O.M. Sopwith against the defender, *Rainbow*, skippered by owner Harold S. Vanderbilt. *Period real photo postcard by Valentine's publishing.*

T. O.M. Sopwith returned in 1937 to capture the elusive Cup with the *Endeavour II*, only to lose four straight races to the super-J the *Ranger*. *Bishop Studio real photo postcard.*

and mast; and a wood Park Avenue boom. She displaced 162 tons. Her loaded waterline length of 87 feet and her overall length of 135.8 gave her the greatest length of all the Js built before her. She twice lost her mast during the 1936 trials preparing for the 1937 challenge. After her defeat in the Cup races, she was laid up at Camper & Nicholson and later sold to reclaim her keel for its lead. The scavenged hulk was broken up in 1968.

## VELSHEDA

The *Velsheda* was the only J-boat not designed to compete for the America's Cup. This steel-masted yacht reused much material from the *White Heather II*'s keel, modified in 1935. Terry Brabant restored the yacht in 1983, maintaining the integrity of her original condition. After sailing as a charter, she became the property of a Swiss owner, and her refit was stalled for lack of funds. Sold in 1996, a major refit was undertaken in 1996–97 at Southampton Yacht Services under Gerard Dykstra, modernizing the boat but making it less authentic.

## VANITIE, A 1920 DEFENDER CANDIDATE

The *Vanitie* lost to the *Resolute* in the 1914 trials (Cup races postponed) and the 1920 trials, losing 7–4 in the final 1920 selection series. She acted as a trial horse in the 1930 and 1934 America's Cup defender trials and was eventually laid up at the Herreshoff yard, where she was scrapped in 1938.

## THE RESOLUTE SUCCESSFULLY DEFENDS THE CUP

The *Resolute*, designed by Nat Herreshoff in 1914 and built at the Herreshoff Manufacturing Company yard, was not designed as a J but was altered after construction to rate as a J. However, she was not acceptable for the America's Cup as a J-class yacht because of her light weight. The *Resolute*—waterline length 74 feet, 11 inches; overall length 106 feet, 4 inches; beam 21 feet, 11 inches; and draft, 13 feet, 9 inches—won the 1920 Cup challenge against the *Shamrock IV*, 3–2. Converted to a schooner rig after her Cup win, she cruised for pleasure for several years and was scrapped at the Herreshoff yard in 1939.[8]

| Name | Designer | Builder | Built | Year | Years Raced | Scrapped |
|---|---|---|---|---|---|---|
| Resolute | N.G. Herreshoff | Herreshoff | USA | 1914 | 1929, 1930, 1931 | 1939 |
| Vanitie | William Gardner | Geo Lawley & Son, Boston | USA | 1914 | 1929, 1930, 1931, 1932, 1933, 1934 | 1939 |
| Enterprise | S. Burgess | Herreshoff | USA | 1930 | 1930 | 1935 |
| Weetamoe | Clinton Crane | Herreshoff | USA | 1930 | 1929, 1930, 1931, 1932, 1933, 1936 | 1938 |
| Yankee | Frank Paine | Geo Lawley & Son, Boston | USA | 1930 | 1930, 1934, 1935, 1936, 1937 | 1941 |
| Shamrock V | Charles Nicholson | Camper & Nicholson | UK | 1930 | 1930 | Restored and still sailing |
| Whirlwind | L.F. Herreshoff | Geo Lawley & Son, Boston | USA | 1930 | 1930 | 1935 |
| Rainbow | S. Burgess | Herreshoff | USA | 1934 | 1934, 1936, 1937 | 1940 |
| Endeavour | Charles Nicholson | Camper & Nicholson | UK | 1934 | 1934 | Restored and still sailing |
| Ranger | S. Burgess O. Stephens | Bath Iron Works | USA | 1937 | 1937 | 1941 |
| Endeavour II | Charles Nicholson | Camper & Nicholson | UK | 1936 | 1937 | 1968 |

*Chapter 9*

# SECRETS AND SPIES

N at Herreshoff had a lifelong fear of spies. He lived in constant suspicion of competing boat builders stealing his ideas. So wary was Captain Nat of camera-toting loiterers that he posted armed guards at his Bristol waterfront yard.

The innovative winged keel of 1983 Cup challenger *Australia II* was painted blue to disappear when in the water and was shrouded when out of the water as protection from curious eyes.

Seldom are visitors to the Goetz Custom Sailboat plant admitted; those allowed a tour are subject to a security check and assigned a security escort.

America's Cup spies continue to ply their craft; only their techniques have changed.

Divers hover under water with watertight cameras near a turning mark during trial races; others swim under the docks of opposing yachts hoping to capture images of the shapes of the boats' hulls or keels. Spy teams in small, speedy boats and helicopters with high-resolution cameras monitor rivals' sailing techniques, which are later analyzed on computers ashore.

During the 1992 challenger and defender trials, the Italian team verbalized angrily about American teams' obvious spying. The Americans replied snidely that the Italians were no less guilty of spying than the Kiwis or the French. America[3] Foundation spokesperson Sue Plowden said, "Those who have the money to invest do it. Those who cannot afford it, complain about it."

Bill Koch did not deny that his team was following potential rivals; at a press conference, he strongly defended the practice. He said it was part of the game.

Captain Nat's magnificent sloops, the *Columbia* (1899 and 1901) and the *Constitution* (foreground).

The majority of teams believe surveillance is legitimate. The *America³* helmsman, Buddy Melges, said, "It's a technology race. That's what this whole thing is built on, and you can't tell your scientists and technicians they have to stay home, sit in an enclosed chamber and dream up ideas to make us sailors happy."

Koch went on to say that some competitors went to the extreme of planting moles in one another's organizations.

For the sake of giving height to the security bar, the challenger and defender syndicates agreed that unofficial syndicate boats would stay at least two hundred meters away from other America's Cup boats, and helicopters would stay at least 1,500 feet laterally and 500 feet vertically away from the boats.

*Chapter 10*

# BEAM, KEEL, WEIGHT
# AND TACTICS

W hen in 1983 the *Australia II* broke the sport's longest winning streak
with its innovative winged keel, it started a revolution in America's
Cup yacht design.

## BEAM

Contenders for the 1995 contest all developed yachts with the same basic
twelve-meter design formula, but as the trial dates approached, all began
concentrating on weight and beam.

Dennis Conner's Newport, Rhode Island tactician, Tom Whidden, said
the Cup boats seen gathering for the trials all had similar characteristics.
Most of the designers of the 1995 fleet of challengers and defenders had
come up with their best guesses about what made the design competitive
for this race for the Cup. The direction of designers was to make boats with
narrower beams.

The *America³*, which successfully defended the Cup in 1992, took a cautious
step in narrowing the beam; it was successful for 1992. However, in the fall of
1994, during the America's Cup Class World Championship in San Diego,
the *America³* (aka *Mighty Mary*), with her all-female crew, was decisively beaten
in the ocean races by the aggressive, narrow-beam *One-Australia*.

Crew members of Ted Turner's twelve-meter sloop the *Courageous* struggle to pull down the sail from the mast that snapped during the first leg of a race in the Cup trials off Newport on July 23, 1980. *UPI wire photo.*

Eventually, when a designer figured out the structure of a boat to everybody's satisfaction, a rival design team made aggressive efforts to reduce the boat's structural weight. The skin thickness and weight were controlled by the rules, but the way the framing was done was the designer's choice, and the way the mast step, chain plates and keel combination went on the boat was unregulated.

David Pedrick of Newport, chief designer for team Dennis Conner, remarked that one thing that has improved tremendously with modern technology is the ability to marry the characteristics of the boat to the racing environment. Pedrick recalled that when his team started planning its first International America's Cup Class boat, they had only about one year of sea state and wind data.

Pedrick said, "After that, we went to the design side and from the choice of design characteristics we decided which of those were optimized for San Diego conditions."

Almost everybody's first-generation boat was built to the maximum beam allowable under the rules. Pedrick, Bruce Todter and Bruce Nelson, who composed Conner's design team, concluded that they should be going in the direction of narrower boats.

"We took a small step in that direction with *Stars & Stripes '92* and used that as our baseline design for the new boat," Pedrick said. For lack of money and time, *Stars & Stripes '92* was designed but never built. Pedrick believes the design for *Stars & Stripes '92* was at least on par with *America³* and would have beaten her.

Team New Zealand's *Black Magic 1* and *2*, the *One-Australia* and Chris Dirkson's New Zealand boat *Tutukaka* all opted for narrow beams. The result was the creation of a fleet of ultra-slim fast boats slicing through the frequently rough Pacific Ocean waters. The consequences were exciting races to watch and danger for the boats' crews, especially when two boats converged on opposite tacks at a combined speed of more than twenty knots.

According to Pedrick, "Narrow beam is favorable in rough water. You lose a little righting momentum, but you reduce resistance. That is a very good tradeoff."

Paul Cayard, who skippered the challenger *Il Moro di Venezia* in 1992, joined Dennis Conner on *Stars & Stripes* in 1995. He believed if they could win the start by .15 or .20 of a knot, they could win the Cup.

# KEEL

The December 1956 revised Deed of Gift concerning keels now reads:

> *Centerboard or sliding keel vessels shall always be allowed to compete in any race for this Cup, and no restriction nor limitation whatever shall be placed on the use of such centerboard or sliding keel, nor shall the centerboard or sliding keel be considered a part of the vessel for any purpose of measurement.*

Olin Stephens advanced the standard twelve-meter formula, the standard for the 1958, 1962 and 1964 Cup races, when he redesigned the keel-rudder configuration for the 1967 *Intrepid*. The idea of shortening the keel was the same plan Stephens used when designing his 1964 defender, the *Constellation*. The short keel and separated rudder were original to Stephens in designing the twelve-meter.

Stephens gave the *Intrepid* a more distinct keel and attached a second rudder to the trailing edge. By adding a second rudder on the trailing edge, the keel leeway was minimized; reshaping the keel this way increased the boat's hydrodynamic lift.

He grew the boat with a narrow swelling of the hull running aft from the keel. Stephens called this bulge the "kicker." His solution to accepting the volume of such a narrow, heavy-displacement hull required reducing keel area and giving the *Intrepid* a sweeter line. The idea of the smaller, more efficient keel and reduced lateral plane area made the *Intrepid* more maneuverable in jockeying to the start and tacking.

# WEIGHT

While Tom Blackaller was planning his 1987 San Francisco–based challenger yacht the *R1*, he contracted Alberto Calderon to develop a more radical design than a winged keel for his twelve-meter hull. In order to avoid the tradition of housing ballast in the keel, Calderon enveloped ballast in a large torpedo shape mounted on a short center-located foil-shaped strut. To generate the craft's lift, Calderon placed high-aspect steerable foils at the bow and stern. Being steerable, the foils allowed the helmsman unprecedented control over direction.

Blackaller's yacht made its way to the challenger semifinals, where she fell to Dennis Conner's eventual Cup winner, the *Stars & Stripes*.

The heavier the keel bulb, the more upright the yacht will sail upwind and, therefore, the quicker the yacht will sail. However, for every ounce of weight added to the keel bulb, an equivalent ounce of weight must be subtracted from another part of the boat because the overall weight is limited by regulations to twenty-four tons.

Eric Goetz and his Goetz Custom Sailboats Company are obsessed with the weight of the Cup boats he builds. Goetz's body of technology is available to all of his customers. This technology involves not only an expertise in composites and resins but also techniques for putting the pieces together. He uses a computer to monitor the hull's weight as it is being built.

This obsession with the boat's weight goes so far that any paint or finish sanded off the hull is swept up and weighed. That weight is figured into the computer's calculation.

# TACTICS

Match racing pits one boat against another in a thrilling contest characterized by tactical cunning and daring maneuvers. The game of nautical chess begins well before the starting gun. The yachts begin maneuvering against each other from five to ten minutes before the actual start. The object of the prestart duel is to gain the best position on the line and simultaneously deny one's opponent any advantage.

In a match race, the aim is not to start with the gun but rather ahead of the opposing boat and, if possible, on its wind. Ideally, the best start is one in which your boat might be over the line a fraction of a minute after the starting gun at full speed, with your sails undisturbed by your opponent. In an ideal world, your opponent would be two lengths behind and to the leeward.

This is the reason that, in the minutes before the starting gun, both boats circle each other, trying to get the better wind. The aim is to be positioned close behind the rival boat, thus enhancing the chance of blocking it when it attempts to head back for the starting line. If in the process you can get your boat on the other's wind, then you will have an excellent start as you cross the line.

As soon as the race begins, it is the task of the leading boat to do everything possible to obstruct the progress of her opponent. The trailing challenger maneuvers by frequent tacking to get clear air. The tacking duels are a favorite tactic of the challenger, designed to find clear wind and, with a bit of luck, to cause a fouled sail or other breakdown in the leading boat.

The accomplished tactician and helmsman have several options in their sailing repertoires; one is simply attempting to be first over the start line and control the race. Another tactic is to secure a particular side of the racecourse where the wind is most favorable. A third tactic is to force your opponent into making an illegal maneuver for which he must pay a penalty, costing valuable time.

*Chapter 11*

# STILL SHIPSHAPE 'N' BRISTOL FASH'N

## Eric Goetz

On an April 1995 evening, boat builder Eric Goetz was addressing a gathering of boating enthusiasts in the Herreshoff Marine Museum when a person asked how he had managed to secure a monopoly on America's Cup boat-building contracts.

Goetz replied, "Basically, I was sitting around about 1989, and I wrote myself a little note saying that if I was going to join an elite group of boat builders, I had to get into the America's Cup. I didn't realize that I would get everything in the America's Cup."

As time passed, Goetz's reputation for reliability and being a builder of dependable, seaworthy boats spread throughout the industry. Eventually, Goetz Custom Sailboats swept away the competition in America's Cup boat building. With a dedicated crew of thirty-two, Goetz serviced all three America's Cup syndicates in 1995. Since 1991, Goetz has built six America's Cup boats.

The Goetz enterprise began in 1975. He started working with Dennis Conner in 1980, when Conner was sailing the *Freedom*; that year, he built a whole series of rudders for Conner, and in 1983, he received another large rudder order. Goetz has developed a long-lasting business and personal friendship with Conner.

Bill Koch is also a Goetz customer of long standing. Goetz Custom Sailboats has built a solid reputation with Koch, for whom it has built boats and test-tank models. In 1992, Koch commissioned the Goetz crew to build the *America³*. Koch spent a lot of time looking for other boat builders but found none with whom he felt comfortable.

A problem arose, however. Goetz had already begun work on Conner's boat, the *Stars & Stripes '92*. To solve the problem, Goetz set up two shops located a half mile apart to service both clients.

Goetz Custom Sailboats has access to many different technologies outside of boats. In 1992, the company worked closely with the Department of Aeronautics and Astrophysics at Stanford University and its laboratory, developing laminating techniques and controls for the laminating ovens. This gave the company a window into other major types of technology that many companies in other countries did not have available.

"American syndicates are funny," Goetz told his audience. "Each one seems to have a car associated with it, and these car companies are very interested in composites, so their laboratories are open to us."

In 1992, Goetz had to prove to the syndicates that he could build their boats without tipping their secrets. In 1995, the company was trusted to do that and could get on with building boats.

The Goetz team pays particular attention to every aspect of security, including to whom it speaks and what leftover pieces of materials it discards as trash and what it destroys. Thus, security and discretion are part of what keeps Goetz on top of the heap of American boat builders. "We've never had a problem," Goetz said, "and the syndicates have found we never have a problem; otherwise, they wouldn't have come back."

In early January 1995, when a tornado tossed one of his boats around a San Diego harbor and put two huge holes in the hull, the two holes were big enough for a man to crawl through. Goetz, who was in San Francisco at the time, flew immediately to San Diego and began the difficult repair task, which took nearly a week of sixteen-hour days. Goetz, with six members of his Bristol team, got the boat shipshape again and returned her to the water.

Goetz said, "Designers always want extra time to design. They say, 'Give us another couple of weeks, and we'll have the faster shape.' They'll keep going until we finally have to rip the plans out of their arms."

At the end of May 1995, a joint venture was announced by Goetz Custom Sailboats of Bristol, Rhode Island, and Derecktor Shipyards (formerly of Newport, Rhode Island)[9] in Mamaroneck, New York. Goetz emphasized that the business enterprise was not a merger; neither company would lose its identity. Each would continue to do its own projects. Goetz would continue building racing boats and America's Cup and Whitbread (around-the-world racers) boats; Derecktor would still build aluminum cruisers, ferryboats and so on. Together, the companies would sometimes build high-tech luxury yachts. At the time the Bristol and Mamaroneck companies entered into their agreement, Goetz was building three America's Cup Class boats for Bill Koch, Dennis Conner and the PACT 95 team.

In August, the partners began construction of their first DG boat, a Sparkman & Stephens–designed seventy-five-foot, fast, luxury, family-weekend-type boat. The hull, deck and interior structures were the responsibility of the Goetz plant on Broad Common Road, and Derecktor's contribution to the project was the lightweight joiner and finish work.

In mid-October 1994, the newly minted eighty-foot hull of *Stars & Stripes '95* dominated the spotless workshop of Goetz Custom Sailboats as the final coats of paint dried.

Less than a half mile away at the boatyard's annex, another Goetz crew was completing Dennis Conner's competitor, *Young America*, for the PACT (Partnership for America's Cup Technology) '95 syndicate. As soon as the *Stars & Stripes* left for San Diego, construction began on another America's Cup hull for Bill Koch—the *Mighty Mary* for the all-female crew.

In a sport of veiled keels and technology espionage, one boatyard found itself entrusted with building all three American competitors. The *Stars & Stripes* skipper, Dennis Conner, said he saw "nothing unusual" about Goetz's monopoly on the America's Cup.

"He has the most experience," said Conner. "Eric has such a high degree of integrity; I'm willing to take the risk."

Thomas L. Stark, chief financial officer for PACT '95, explained, "Eric Goetz is an incredibly talented boat builder who delivers the boat on time, on budget and on spec. He is a good businessman, straightforward, very professional; that sets him apart from the bulk of the industry."

Goetz builds hulls of competing yachts at separate facilities. Doors are always closed, and when visitors are allowed, they are escorted and issued security badges. Goetz and all his employees are required to sign confidentiality agreements with the syndicates. The company's "security code" is not burdensome. The company developed the procedures back in 1991, when Goetz first found himself in the position of building boats for two competitors, Dennis Conner and Bill Koch; the Goetz-built *America³* eventually won the Cup in 1992.

In early August 1995, the 15-foot bulbed keel and 110-foot mast of the America's Cup Class yacht the *Defiant* became a towering presence on the Bristol waterfront on a Hope Street lot facing the Herreshoff Marine

Museum. Built by Goetz Custom Sailboats, the *Defiant* was a gift to the America's Cup Hall of Fame from owner Bill Koch. The *Defiant* was built as the prototype of *America³*.

Goetz established his reputation as an excellent custom boat builder before he signed his first America's Cup contract.

By the time Goetz set up his Bristol operation, his team had already built twelve large racing yachts, including the *Vineta*, a thirty-eight-foot Britton Chance design, which became an alternate on the German Admiral's Cup team.

As his name and work became better known, he received honors for his innovations in yacht technology and construction; he began building a series of yachts designed according to the International Offshore Rule.

These included the *Runaway*, designed by Kirby for the Canadian Admiral's Cup team; the forty-one-foot *Thunderbolt*, whose co-designer, Bruce Nelson, has been a member of the last three Dennis Conner design teams; and the forty-three-foot *High Roller*, which was the top-scoring U.S. boat in the 1985 Admiral's Cup races.

In 1989, the Goetz team built its first two maxi boats: *The Card*, a Bruce Farr design, for the Whitbread Round-the-World race; and the *Ermeraude*, for Jacques de Wailly, skippered by Dennis Conner in the 1989 and 1999 world maxi boat championships. In 1990, Goetz built the *Matador²*, a maxi boat Bill Koch took to the world maxi boat championships. Goetz has built more than large high-tech racers; his repertoire also includes several narrow-beam cruising sailboats and racing powerboats.

# HALL SPARS

Hall Spars and Rigging is the premier builder of high-performance carbon-fiber spars and rigging. Beginning in June 1980, Eric Hall and Phil Garland founded their first shop at 7 Burnside Street in Bristol, Rhode Island, on the grounds of the storied Herreshoff Manufacturing Company. Today, in 2012, Hall has four locations on three continents and supplies some of the most recognized Grand Prix programs in the world.

During the 1990s, the bonanza days of America's Cup boat building, nearly two dozen Rhode Island East Bay firms—including Hall Spars, building booms, poles and rigging—reaped America's Cup business.

Eric Hall wrote an informational letter to the *Providence Journal* that appeared in the July 7, 2007 issue. It reads as follows:

*With regard to the July 3 editorial, "America's Cup Big Again?" although it is not completely inaccurate to say that both teams are New Zealand based, Americans are in fact in key positions on both teams. On Alinghi the helmsman is in fact the highly skilled Ed Baird from Florida. His backup is Peter Holmberg from the U.S. Virgin Islands.*

*On the New Zealand boat, both the tactician and navigator, the two most important positions along with the helmsman, are Americans Terry Hutchison and Kevin Hall (no relation). On the design side, Rhode Islander Dirk Kramers is the genius behind Alinghi's innovative hull structures and U.S. Virgin Island native (and recent Rhode Island resident) Kirst Feddersen designed Alinghi's mast and rigging, which were built right here in Bristol by our company Hall Spars, as they were last time around when Alinghi won the Cup.*

*Therefore, it is fair to say that without the "American Connection," these New Zealand based teams would not be the formidable teams that they are.*

*As far as U.S. interest goes, at least we in the sailing community are watching closely, on the edge of our seats, as this drama-packed America's Cup plays out.*

Eric Hall can trace the path leading him to establish his spar-manufacturing company. As a lad, he and his brothers, Ned and Ben, sailed on the family racer-cruisers; he remembers that when he was a high school student, he daydreamed about owning his own business. After high school, in the late 1960s, Eric became a distributor for specialty sailing and rigging gear. In 1972, he took a job managing a spar business in Germany with an option for partnership.

Eric says his guide to succeeding in business was the champion race car driver Bruce McLaren, who, when asked the secret of building better race cars, answered, "No secret at all. We just make common race cars uncommonly well." Eric said he liked that, and to this day, the McLaren way of doing business remains the Hall Spars way.

In 1975, Eric helped start a spar business as a partner with Stearn Mast in Wisconsin. Shortly after, he joined the Schaefer Marine spar business. When Schaefer quit making spars in 1980, he decided the time was right to start his own business and signed a license agreement with Schaefer. The first Hall customers were Tartan Yachts, S2 and Pearson Yachts.

In 1981, Kenyon Marine in Guilford, Connecticut, was the largest spar supplier in the United States, thanks in part to its production of the J/24 mast. Watching with great interest the emergence of Hall Spars was Kenyon's vice-president and soon-to-be-named president Ben Hall, Eric's brother.

Ben recalls that in 1984 he'd had enough with the corporate politics at Kenyon, so it was an easy decision to leave; he joined his brother as Hall Spars co-owner and vice-president.

The first sales call Eric and Ben made together was to Bob and Rod Johnstone at J Boats. For many years, Ben had a convivial relationship with Bob and Rod, so it was a friendly business meeting, the result of which was landing nearly all of J Boats' business.

Ben was winning helmsman on several important races, including the Miami Nassau Race and the Bermuda Race, under Hall masts. Hall's successes started making big impressions on yacht builders. Hall was not a huge manufactory, but it managed to achieve much with very little.

Avid racing sailor Phil Garland had offers to run boatyards in Edgartown, Massachusetts, and Whangarei, New Zealand, but his interest was toward the rigging business. Eric Goetz introduced Phil to Eric Hall; that is the short story of how he became a co-owner of Hall Spars and Rigging.

Within three years, Eric and Phil began soliciting the high-performance racing spar and rigging business, and they began building their first America's Cup mast.

By 1988, the company had outgrown the Herreshoff building; it was then that the team broke ground for a new state-of-the-art building at the Bristol Industrial Park. Eventually, the industrial park grew into a major marine hub, with boat builders Carroll Marine, Goetz Boats, Merrifield Roberts and Shannon Yachts, in addition to Hall, all humming with activity during the 1990s.

Beginning in the new decade of the '90s, Hall Spars's commitment to composites was well established. In 1992, the America$^3$ America's Cup syndicate chose Hall to build its booms, spinnaker poles, reaching struts and rudderstocks. After manufacturing the requested *America$^3$* gear, Hall began receiving increasingly more requests from the syndicate. Not only did the work with America$^3$ put Hall at the top of the sailing industry in carbon fiber technology and manufacturing, but it also established Hall engineering as a force in composite design.

By the time the Cup races concluded, Hall's transition to carbon was complete. In 1994, Hall was building the first carbon spars for one-design production boats: the J/120 and J/130. That same year, Hall built the first composite spar for a production IMS racer, Carroll Marine's Nelson Marek 39, and custom racing masts for the Nelson Marek fifty-footer *Virago* and Tripp 49 *Wonder*.

For the next Cup in 1995, Hall built composite structural elements, as well as a boom, for the Young America's Cup defense bid. Though unsuccessful in defending the Cup, the Young America syndicate was back with another Cup bid in 1999, and Hall Spars built a radical wing-shaped mast. The three-spreader rig was very stiff, with the largest fore-and-aft dimension of any mast in Auckland, adding considerable unrated sail area. It was very fast, and it caught the attention of young Russell Coutts, New Zealand's skipper.

When Russell Coutts left the New Zealand team, moving to the Swiss team *Alinghi*, he contracted Hall Spars to build the spars for his new renegade team. In March 2003, the *Alinghi*, equipped with a Hall mast, boom, reaching strut and spinnaker pole, won the America's Cup.

The finish of the Volvo Round-the-World Ocean Race in 2006 marked the beginning of the next America's Cup cycle. Hall products were in high demand, and construction began on masts for four America's Cup teams preparing for the 2007 races: *Alinghi*, *Luna Rossa*, *Mascalzone Latino* and *Victory Challenge*.

In June 2007, the *Alinghi* won a second America's Cup outfitted with Hall Spars equipment. As of this writing, Hall has built spars for six America's Cup yachts, four of them winners.

*Chapter 12*

# THE 1980 CHALLENGE

*A Challenger and Defender Overview*

## THE CHALLENGER: *SVERIGE*

The designer of the *Sverige*, a traditional twelve-meter yacht, used the *Courageous* as his inspiration. Since being a contestant in the 1977 challenger trial races, the *Sverige* received many upgrades—her mast, rig and sails were improved, her winches were changed and her deck layout was modified.

Sails were the biggest problem in 1977. No more than two sails functioned properly; the computerized curves on which the *Sverige* relied did not work as well as expected.

The Swedish yacht *Sverige* is seen going through her paces during the July 30, 1980 Louis Vuitton Cup Challenger Selection Series in Newport. *UPI wire photo.*

She sailed into Newport for the 1980 Louis Vuitton Cup Challenger Selection Series as a radically improved contender.

## THE CHALLENGER: *AUSTRALIA*

The *Australia* proved not to be what she used to be. Her underwater line had increased with a longer keel; she had a new deeper and thinner rudder and a new delta-formed mast. In 1977, some critics who watched closely believed

she was using American rigging, winches and sails.

Others believed the Australian crew was probably the most experienced among all the challengers in the 1980 Cup matches. Their experience included 1974, when they challenged with the *Southern Cross*, and 1977, when they challenged with the *Australia*. During the autumn of 1979, the *Australia* sailed several times against the *Gretel II*.

The *Australia* is testing her sails and readying her crew in preparation for the best-of-seven Cup series in Rhode Island Sound. *UPI wire photo dated September 14, 1980.*

## THE CHALLENGER: *LIONHEART*

The *Lionheart* was a conventional twelve-meter yacht designed by Ian Howlett; she had a cut-off freeboard and a relatively low and sharp bow that required him to cut back elsewhere to make sure the measurements added up to twelve.

Helmsman John Oakely selected his sails with an eye to having less pressure on the mast and at the stern. He designed his mainsails with double cloth at the stern and a lighter, simpler cloth forward.

Compared with the Swedes, the British syndicate was financially weak. However, the *Lionheart* proved to be a fast boat and a very competitive sailor.

## THE DEFENDER: *ENTERPRISE*

The Olin Stephens–designed *Enterprise* was a contender as a Cup defender in 1977. However, in the 1977 trials, she was defeated by the *Courageous*, forcing her into second place as a defender candidate. The *Enterprise* was the biggest of the twelves in Newport in 1977; she measured sixty-seven feet compared to the *Sverige*'s sixty-three feet.

Lowell North and Dennis Conner shared the *Enterprise*'s helm. Conner's agreement with the West Coast syndicate was that he could move from boat to boat as long as in the end he settled on a winning contender. Conner did eventually find the winner in the Fort Schuyler Foundation–financed *Freedom*.

## THE DEFENDER: *COURAGEOUS*

In 1977, Ted Turner chartered the *Courageous*. Folks in the know gave him little chance of qualifying in competition with the *Enterprise*, the *Intrepid* and the *Independence*. However, Turner did sail the *Courageous* from one victory to another against all competitors, and he was determined to sail the *Courageous* as Cup defender.

Ted Turner's twelve-meter yacht the *Courageous* lost her mast while sailing against Russell Long's *Clipper* in the first leg of the July 23, 1980 race in the Cup defender trials. David Pedrick designed the *Clipper* with keel, rig, sails and steering gear salvaged from the *Independence*. *UPI wire photo by Jerry Taylor.*

*Above*: Ted Turner's potential Cup defender the *Courageous* had her bow lengthened with the hope of increasing her speed in the mid-August defender selection trials. As of August 1, 1980, the *Courageous* had the worst record—five wins and twenty-two losses—of the three American yachts vying for the privilege to defend the Cup. *UPI wire photo.*

*Left*: The Cup defender *Freedom* is hauled out at the Williams & Manchester Shipyard in Newport on September 15, 1980, for minor repairs and painting one day before the official start of the best-four-out-of-seven America's Cup series. *UPI wire photo.*

Now known as "Captain Courageous," Turner won the 1977 match, sinking the *Australia* 4–0.

However, as hard as he tried, it turned out differently in 1980. Turner lost the defender trials to Dennis Conner and the *Freedom*, which went on to save the Cup, winning 4–1 over the *Australia*.

# The Defender: *Freedom*

The *Freedom* was another Olin Stephens–designed masterpiece; however, in appearance, the *Freedom* was unremarkable. Stephens was not interested in elegance; the underwater body design held no secrets. He was more concerned with cutting down weight and air resistance. Thus, he created a broad foreship and extremely low freeboard. Unlike the *Enterprise*, the *Freedom* had two steering wheels.

The West Coast Enterprise syndicate named Conner first skipper and gave him a free hand. During the defender trials, Conner's goal was to out sail Ted Turner and keep him off balance. The eventual outcome of the trials and the Cup races is well known.

*Chapter 13*

# 1983 AUSTRALIA'S CUP

The *Australia II* skipper John Bertrand and syndicate head Alan Bond representing the Royal Perth Yacht Club of Western Australia both predicted an Australian victory. Bond predicted the Aussies to win the Cup match, 4–2. Bond did not predict a sweep but did say his yacht would win four races. Bertrand sounded an equally optimistic note. "I think we're near a level of performance which hasn't been attained by any Australian challenger before," he said.

The Australian boat and the *Liberty*, representing the New York Yacht Club, launched the best-of-seven series for the America's Cup on September 13, 1983. Both boats got out early to the America's Cup buoy 7.9 miles southeast of the Brenton Reef Light, where all the races in this series started.

The U.S. Coast Guard mustered a fleet of eight cutters, eighteen forty-one-foot patrol boats, ten Coast Guard auxiliary craft and the destroyer USS *Edson* to handle the expected large spectator fleet. The Coast Guard was involved in keeping all the spectator craft off the diamond-shaped restricted racecourse on Rhode Island Sound.

Most everyone who is familiar with the intricacies of sailboat match racing, including the sailors involved, agree that this match had rapidly become a contest of nationalities, a world championship contest not only between sailors but also between yacht designers, builders, sail makers, mast and winch makers and, most recently, computer designers.

Before the two boats reached their first mark, four and a half miles from the starting line, sports handicappers had a good idea whether the Cup

The challenger yacht *Australia*'s crew and her skipper, Jim Hardy (waving, right), appear relaxed while being towed to the race area off Newport on September 16, 1980, for the first race in the Cup series against the Cup defender *Freedom*. *UPI wire photo.*

would stay at the New York Yacht Club for another four years or be going "Down Under" to Australia.

The race was on, and the boat with the finest tactics and the secret keel won.

The boat-handling techniques of sailing the *Australia II* were completely new to a twelve-meter. Because the *Australia II* turned quickly and accelerated much faster than conventional twelves when maneuvering, she had new and potentially superior tactics. In the first two races against the *Liberty*, however, Bertrand was unable to use his boat's maneuvering superiority to his advantage, but all that changed by the end of the series, and he won the last three races.

The momentous loss of the America's Cup by the New York Yacht Club was the most closely sailed match in the history of the event, and the excitement went down to the final race.

Alan Bond's years of effort finally paid off, and he took the Victorian-era trophy, claimed by the Americans 132 years earlier, to a new home at the Royal Perth Yacht Club in Perth, Western Australia.

Dennis Conner and the *Liberty* won the first two races and John Bertrand and the *Australia II* the third. The Americans recovered in the fourth but knew they were in trouble in light air. The two-race American lead faded to a 3–3 tie by the end of the sixth race. In the fifth leg of the final race, Bertrand steered the *Australia II* from a fifty-seven-second deficit to a forty-one-second lead at the final mark.

By the end of the seventh race, the Cup was heading to Australia, the "Thunder from Down Under" finishing forty-one seconds ahead of the *Liberty* and ending the longest winning streak in the history of sport.

| Race Date | Yacht | Winning Time |
|---|---|---|
| September 13 | *Liberty* | 1 minute, 10 seconds |
| September 15 | *Liberty* | 1 minute, 33 seconds |
| September 17 | *Australia II* | 3 minutes, 14 seconds |
| September 18 | *Liberty* | 43 seconds |
| September 19 | *Australia II* | 1 minute, 47 seconds |
| September 22 | *Australia II* | 3 minutes, 25 seconds |
| September 26 | *Australia II* | 41 seconds |

# Chapter 14

# THE 1992 MATCH

*America³ v. Il Moro di Venezia*

The Twenty-eighth America's Cup contest between the winner of the 1992 Citizen Cup Defender Selection Series, Bill Koch's San Diego Yacht Club boat the *America³*, and the winner of the 1992 Louis Vuitton Cup Challenger Selection Series, Italy's Compagnia Della Vela di Venezia *Il Moro di Venezia*, proved to be the closest race in the America's Cup history.

## THE DEFENDER TRIALS

### *January 14, 1992*

The Citizen Cup defender selection race for the Twenty-eighth America's Cup match proved not to be a cut-and-dried affair. For that, the America's Cup Organizing Committee was very pleased.

In a sailing scuffle between Dennis Conner and Bill Koch, Conner, who had so much success in all kinds of racing yachts, appeared as the decisive favorite. But it proved that Conner had a real fight on his hands from Koch and his crack team of America's Cup sailors on the *Defiant* and the *Jayhawk*, two of Koch's four entries.

Koch's skipper Buddy Melges, tactician Dave Dellenbaugh and the *Defiant* crew proved they could match tacks and tactics with Conner and his crew of Cup veterans.

Conner put his *Stars & Stripes* across the starting line six seconds ahead of the *Defiant*, but he quickly found himself on the wrong side of the course, and when the boats came together for the first time, the *Defiant* had gained significantly.

The *Defiant* led at every mark on the eight-leg 22.6-mile course on the Pacific Ocean. Conner twice closed the gap, but the *Defiant* blew away the *Stars & Stripes* at the end of the final upwind leg en route to a winning margin of one minute, thirty-four seconds corrected time.

## January 15, 1992

When the race started, the waters off Point Loma looked like the waters in Rhode Island Sound after a strong cold front had passed through. California native Dennis Conner used the fluky San Diego wind to his advantage. The wind was blowing, and if not vigilant, one's strategy in a sailboat race would be violently disrupted. That is what happened to Bill Koch and his *Jayhawk* crew of East Coast sailors in the second race of the defender trials.

The wind kept shifting through the first six legs of the course, and Conner's *Stars & Stripes* was always on the leading edge of the shifts and best able to take advantage of them. Conner won the second defender trial race by four minutes, ten seconds.

## January 18, 1992

The race began in winds of four to five knots that freshened briefly during the first leg but faded to a barely discernible breeze at the race's end.

The *Defiant* defeated Dennis Conner's *Stars & Stripes* for the second time in the fourth race of the opening round of defender trials. The *Defiant*'s margin of victory over the 22.6-mile, eight-leg course was three minutes, forty-six seconds.

## January 19, 1992

The *Stars & Stripes* defeated the *Jayhawk* for the second time, winning by two minutes, sixteen seconds in the fifth of nine races.

Bill Koch tenaciously battled Conner for the first six legs of the eight-leg course before Conner broke away for good on the seventh leg. Conner never trailed after taking a two-second lead at the start.

## January 22, 1992

The *Defiant* and the *Stars & Stripes* put on a classic match race evocative of the twelve-meter racing in Newport and Fremantle.

Near the end of the sixth leg, Conner luffed the *Stars & Stripes* sharply to prevent the *Defiant* from getting by him to windward.

Buddy Melges, sailing the *Defiant*, responded to the luff and then called "mast abeam," meaning he thought he was even with the mast of the other boat.

Melges bore off. Conner did the same, and both boats raised red- and yellow-striped protest flags. The umpires waved a green flag, indicating no foul, and the race went on to an eventual win by the *Defiant* by fifty seconds.

## *January 23, 1992*

With the first round of defender trials over, the big winner was Bill Koch, mastermind of the *America³* syndicate's high-tech, four-boat and $64 million quest for the Cup.

Koch was beaten badly in the *Jayhawk* (0–5), losing every outing against teammate Buddy Melges in the *Defiant* (5–0) and Conner in the *Stars & Stripes* (3–3). Melges's undefeated string and flawless sailing performances knocked Conner from the rank of favorite.

## *February 8–9, 1992*

On Saturday, skipper Conner lost to Koch's new *America³* by 6:22.00 and to Koch's *Defiant* on Sunday by 4:16.00. Pushed by southeasterly twelve- to fifteen-knot winds off Point Loma, the *Defiant* cruised around the course in 2:37.38. The *Stars & Stripes*' only wins were against the *Jayhawk*, which Koch retired at the end of round one.

## *February 10, 1992*

The *Defiant*'s first loss in the defender selection series was a victory—a victory for *America³* the boat and America³ the syndicate.

The America³ Foundation's newest boat, also named *America³*, was launched on February 3. She quickly won her first two races, defeating her older stable mate, the *Defiant*, on Monday in race number three of the second round robin of the series.

## *February 11, 1992*

Bill Koch's *America³* extended her winning streak to three in a row, handing Conner's beleaguered *Stars & Stripes* an embarrassing six-minute loss in the fourth race of round two of the defender selection series.

The *America³* trailed the *Stars & Stripes* by five seconds at the start but quickly took command of the race, completing the eight-leg, 22.6-mile race in two hours, forty-two minutes and fifty-five seconds.

## February 13, 1992

With strategist John Bertrand at the helm, the *Stars & Stripes* defeated the *Defiant* by fifty-five seconds for the first time in five tries.

The *Stars & Stripes* trailed the *Defiant* by as much as one minute and then tenaciously fought back for a come-from-behind victory in the fifth race of round two of the Cup defender trials.

Credited for the win was the introduction of a new keel, rudder and mast combination installed the night before the race.

## March 3, 1992

Dennis Conner was trying everything in his racing book to keep up with Bill Koch's four boat–rich campaign to defend the America's Cup.

Conner said he planned to continue with his basic boat. He raced with a radical tandem-keel in part of round two. His designers placed a double keel and a lead bulb on the *Stars & Stripes* and eliminated its conventional rudder. The configuration caused the boat to sideslip during racing.

With winds shifting from the southeast at about twelve to fourteen knots, Conner hoisted a gennaker that produced a powerful surge in the fourth leg of the course, which shaved forty-five seconds off a one-hour-and-two-minute *America³* lead.

The Koch boat regained its lead by the seventh leg and sailed over the finish line with a respectable lead.

## March 4, 1992

The *Stars & Stripes* made it three in a row over the the *Defiant* by two minutes, fifteen seconds.

The *Defiant,* with Buddy Melges at the helm, held a fifteen-second lead at the end of the first leg of the eight-leg course, but the *Stars & Stripes* capitalized on a broken spinnaker pole aboard the *Defiant* and moved into the lead.

The *Defiant*'s fate was sealed when the foredeck crew was slow in switching from a gennaker to a genoa jib, which allowed the *Stars & Stripes* to pull away to a one-minute-and-thirteen-second lead.

The genoa jib, a triangular-shaped headsail, was not properly trimmed for several minutes while the *Defiant's* crew struggled to take down the huge gennaker, which is an asymmetrical spinnaker used when sailing off the wind. The gennaker became tangled in the rigging, holding up the boat's 110-foot mast.

## March 9, 1992

Conner's *Stars & Stripes* was dealt a setback when the boat's 110-foot mast broke at about the 30-foot point and came crashing to the deck as the powerful spinnaker was being set for a downwind run against the *America³*. The Koch boat, leading by thirty-five seconds when Conner's mast came down, only had to complete the course to collect the victory.

## April 12, 1992

Bill Koch's *America³* won its fifth straight race to advance to the defender finals after Koch's fourth boat, the *Kanza*,[10] left the race because she developed a crack in a structural bulkhead that supports the mast ram, the hydraulic ram that controls the position of the mast at the deck and the boat's keel.

## April 13, 1992

Dennis Conner kept alive his chance to sail in five Cup finals by beating the *Kanza* by two minutes, twelve seconds.

Monday's moderate wind, ranging from six to eleven knots, favored the *Stars & Stripes*. As the wind dropped, Conner reached the weather mark four minutes and nine seconds ahead of the *Kanza*. The *Stars & Stripes* turned her run of bad luck around with two straight victories to clinch second place in the semifinals.

## April 30, 1992

Bill Koch's *America³* reached the brink of winning the defender finals with a one-minute- and forty-three-second victory over Conner's *Stars & Stripes* with a 6–4 lead in the best-of-thirteen trials.

The *America³* sliced through the choppy water more easily than the *Stars & Stripes*, pointing higher, footing faster and working out to a one-minute- and eight-second lead at the first mark.

## May 1, 1992

Koch's *America³* snuffed out Conner's hopes of defending the Cup for an unprecedented sixth time when it sunk the *Stars & Stripes* by five minutes eight seconds into the eleventh race in what proved to be the final race of the defenders' finals.

## THE CHALLENGER TRIALS

Eight challengers from seven nations contested the 1992 Louis Vuitton Cup races held in San Diego. Together they spent over $250 million. Il Moro di Venezia alone constructed four boats and spent over $85 million. The winner, *Il Moro di Venezia*, went on to challenge for the 1992 America's Cup.

## January 28, 1992

Prerace favorite *Il Moro di Venezia* sailed the wrong heading on the third leg of the eight-leg course and lost to the *Nippon* by three minutes, fifty-five seconds in the third race of the challenger selection series.

In the other matchups on January 28, France's *Ville de Paris* dispatched Spain's *Espana '92* by six minutes and twenty-four seconds, the *Spirit of Australia* routed Sweden's *Tre Kronor* by thirteen minutes and thirteen seconds and the *New Zealand* beat the *Challenge Australia* by five minutes and three seconds.

In the prerace jousting, *Il Moro* skipper Paul Cayard aggressively chased the *Nippon* around the staging area behind the starting line. At one point, the *Nippon*, skippered by Chris Dickson, with the right of way over Cayard, failed to maintain his course, almost causing a collision between the two seventy-five-foot sloops.

## February 19, 1992

The *New Zealand* maintained its round-two lead in the challenger selection series by defeating Italy's *Il Moro* by one minute, sixteen seconds.

On this date, the *New Zealand*'s record improved to 10–1; *Il Moro*, now 8–2, dropped to third place behind Japan's *Nippon* (9–2). The *New Zealand*'s only loss was to *Il Moro* in the first round.

The *Nippon* overcame kelp on its keel and a broken spinnaker halyard in topping the winless *Challenge Australia* by three minutes and thirty-three seconds. The *Nippon* stopped dead in the water at the fourth mark, while two crew members jumped into the water to clear the kelp.

That allowed the *Challenge Australia* to pass the *Nippon* and take the lead. The *Nippon* soon regained the lead when the *Challenge Australia* dropped a sail in the water and took several minutes to recover it.

France's *Ville de Paris* set back Spain's *Espana '92* by three minutes and seven seconds and moved into fourth place; the *Espana* dropped to sixth place.

The *Spirit of Australia* defeated Sweden's *Tre Kronor* by two minutes and fifty-two seconds, taking over fifth place with a record of 5–6. The *Sweden*, at 1–10, was in seventh place, and the *Challenge Australia*, with no wins, was eighth.

## *April 30, 1992*

The Italians and their American-born skipper, Paul Cayard, were the winners of the Louis Vuitton Cup and the official America's Cup challengers.

*Il Moro* wrapped it up with a one-minute-and-thirty-three-second victory, winning the best of nine series 5–3.

In the last few races, the Italians were superior in tactics, and in eleven to fourteen knots of wind and lumpy seas, they ran away from the *New Zealand*, especially on the windward legs.

## THAT COVETED CUP

Bill Koch, who mounted an eighteen-month, $65 million campaign, was crowned with success when his Bristol-built carbon-fiber racer the *America³* beat the Italian boat *Il Moro*, winning the twenty-eighth match for the America's Cup four wins to one.

The margin of victory in the five races averaged forty seconds, making it the closest racing in America's Cup history.

The Italians dogged the Americans all the way around the course, despite breaking two battens on their mainsail before the race even started and blowing out a spinnaker on the first downwind leg. Later, the Italian boat made up significant ground on the American boat on the close-reaching leg and on the last windward leg, where Koch gave the helm back to Melges, whom Koch was heard to call "one of the best, if not the best, sailors in the world."

As they crossed the line, both Koch and Melges held the steering wheel, and then the backup team came to join them for the happy sail back to the San Diego Yacht Club.

*Chapter 15*

# THE 1995 MATCH

*Black Magic v. Young America*

For the twenty-ninth Cup defense, five nations sent seven syndicates to San Diego, each team with the hopes of capturing the renowned Cup.

By agreement with the PACT 95 syndicate, Dennis Conner was allowed to shift the crew from his *Stars & Stripes* to *Young America* for the best-of-nine series against New Zealand's *Black Magic*.

Conner and handicappers felt that the *Stars & Stripes* could not match the speed of the *Black Magic*, which had lost only one race in four months of competitions in the challenger trials.

Conner said, "*Stars & Stripes* brought us to where we are today. However, four months of defender trials have proven the *Young America*'s hull has speed advantages. This boat and the proven strengths of the *Stars & Stripes* team will be a winning combination in the America's Cup [races]."[11]

David Pedrick, the principal designer of the *Stars & Stripes*, sharply criticized the San Diego Yacht Club and the America's Cup Defense Committee for allowing Conner to switch to the *Young America* for the finals.

Likewise, Peter Blake, head of the challenging New Zealand syndicate, criticized the defense committee.

"We realize coming here to San Diego the rules were going to be changed, that if you can't win by fair means, change the rules and see what you can get away with," Blake said.

After close competition on the first two legs in choppy seas, the *Young America* fell behind the *Black Magic*, losing the first match on May 5 to the Kiwi challenger by two minutes, forty-five seconds.

Kiwi skipper Russell Coutts had been sailing his boat for five months and had no difficulty doing many things instinctively.

Conversely, Conner, his helmsman Paul Cayard, his tactician Tom Whidden and the rest of the crew were still trying to become acquainted with their boat because steering wheels, runner winches and other gear were in unaccustomed positions.

Sportswriter Dave Philips wrote in his May 9 *Providence Journal-Bulletin* article:

> *New Zealand's* Black Magic *was a rocket ship in smooth seas and 7-to-9-knot winds yesterday, as it walloped the defender* Young America *by 4 minutes and 14 seconds for a 2–0 lead in the best-of-nine series.*
>
> *It was the worst defeat for an American defender since* Columbia *lost to the British challenger* Livonia *by 15 minutes and 10 seconds in 1871.*

The *Black Magic*'s speed continued to prove superior to the *Young America*. It was especially outstanding going into the wind. The Kiwi boat gained 0:41, 0:48 and 2:03 on upwind legs and lost some of its lead on two of the three downwind legs. The challenger's keel, with wider wings set farther back than the wings on the defender's keel, was a big help going into the wind.

The *Young America* forced the *Black Magic* off the right side of the course in the prestart maneuvering and won the start for the second race, a two-second lead that proved insignificant. The Kiwis started up the right side of the course, caught a favorable wind shift and took the lead just five minutes into the race; they never trailed again.

Dennis Conner and team *Stars & Stripes* lost their third straight race aboard the *Young America* to challenger *Black Magic* on May 9.

For the second time in the three struggles, Paul Cayard, steering the *Young America*, got the best of the start, forcing the *Black Magic* to tack away on port, and Cayard hit the starting line with better speed, going left.

In those first few minutes, a left-hand shift in the wind might have put the *Young America* in a strong leading position. However, the wind went the other way, and although Cayard was able to engage the Kiwis in a downwind tacking duel halfway up the leg, he was unable to break through against them.

The Kiwis' margin of victory—one minute, fifty-one seconds—was the smallest in the series thus far. A new and more efficient mainsail on *Young America* and winds up to sixteen knots suited the defender better than the conditions in the two previous races.

Race four was an embarrassment to Conner and his hardworking weathered crew with a defeat of three minutes, thirty-seven seconds by the New Zealanders.

Race five was a closer finish—one minute, fifty seconds—but Conner now had the distinction of being the only defending skipper in America's Cup history who lost the Cup on two occasions, this time by a humiliating five straight losses.

The *Black Magic* easily defeated Dennis Conner's *Stars & Stripes* team, 5–0, to win the Cup for New Zealand. Although team *Young America*'s Cup candidate yacht, the *USA-36*, was defeated in defender trials by the *Stars & Stripes*' *USA-34*, the San Diego Yacht Club elected to defend the Cup with the *USA-36* crewed by *Stars & Stripes* sailors.

It is reasonable to salute and admire the Kiwi sailors and the *Black Magic* yacht, which won forty-one races in forty-three attempts in the trials beginning in January; in the actual Cup match, they led at all thirty marks and made up time on twenty-five of thirty legs.

The run-up to the 1995 Cup was notable for the televised sinking of *One Australia* during the fourth round robin of the Louis Vuitton challenger selection series, with all hands escaping uninjured. The 1995 defender selection series also had the first (almost) all-female (with one male) crew sailing Bill Koch's yacht *USA-43*, the *Mighty Mary*.

*Chapter 16*

# THE 2010 MATCH

*Alinghi5 v. BMW Oracle*

The Swiss team sailing the *Alinghi* defeated the 2003 defender, New Zealand's *Black Magic*, and in 2007 successfully defended the Cup against a reconditioned *Black Magic*.

The Nautical Society of Geneva sponsored the Swiss defender, the *Alinghi5*. Because Switzerland has no natural access to the ocean, Valencia acted again as the race site for the 2010 races.

The racecourse in the Mediterranean off Valencia, Spain, varied for each of the three planned races of the thirty-third running for custody of the America's Cup. The first race consisted of a twenty-mile run to windward and a return to the starting point. The plan for the second race was an equilateral-triangle course consisting of thirteen nautical miles on each leg.

The Swiss boat's skipper, Brad Butterworth, a New Zealander sailing in his fifth America's Cup race, boasted a tactician winning in 1995 and 2000 on the *Black Magic* and in 2003 and 2007 on the *Alinghi*.

This year's defender, the *Alinghi5*, a catamaran measuring 90 feet in waterline length and 115 feet overall, met the American challenger, the *BMW Oracle*.

The *BMW Oracle*, hosted by the San Diego Golden Gate Yacht Club, was the only challenger for possession of the eminent Cup. The American *USA 17* was a trimaran of 90 feet waterline length and 113 feet overall, with a metallic wing-type sail rather than a usual fabric mainsail.

The American team's captain, New Zealander Russell Coutts, had skippered a winning Cup boat in three of four previous Cup matches, winning for the *Alinghi* in 2003 and for team New Zealand in 1995 and 2000.

Interestingly, New Zealanders Brad Butterworth and Russell Coutts were team members on the *Black Magic* in 1995 and 2000 and on the *Alinghi* in 2003. For the 2010 match, they were opponents.

Before the actual start of the first race, the combatants dueling for the most advantageous position held the spectator fleet's rapt attention. The *Alinghi5* made a tactical error by not keeping clear and received a penalty. Then, a half minute before the starting gun, the *BMW Oracle* made a mistake, stalling above the starting line and letting the defender cross the line with a substantial lead. However, that was the only time the *Alinghi5* had the lead. The *BMW Oracle* quickly gained the lead, and at the mark twenty miles upwind, she was three minutes, twenty-one seconds ahead. The *Alinghi5* lost more time on the race home during a penalty turn. The challenger won the first match by fifteen minutes, twenty-eight seconds.

At the beginning of race two, it appeared that this might be a close race. The *Alinghi5* received a penalty before the start but took advantage of wind shifts and cunning strategy and led to the lay line, where both yachts had to tack for the first upwind mark. To avoid tacking right in front of the challenger, the *Alinghi5* was forced to sail far above the mark. The *BMW Oracle* took advantage of this and gained the lead, rounding the first mark twenty-two seconds ahead. From this point, it was all speed all the way up the second leg, a reach, hitting an average of thirty-three knots and increasing its lead to two minutes, forty-four seconds.

The challenger captured the Cup in a sprint to the finish, winning by five minutes, twenty-three seconds. Because the *BMW Oracle* won the first two in the best-of-three contest, only two races were run.

# HISTORICAL CHRONOLOGY

1851      The sloop *America* wins against the British squadron; there is no second place.

1870      The *Cambria*, the British challenger, loses against fourteen New York Yacht Club yachts in New York Harbor. The *Magic* is the winner of record.

1871      The New York Yacht Club uses two yachts, the *Columbia* and the *Sappho*, and defeats the English boat *Livonia*.

1876      The *Madeleine* defeats the Canadian *Countess of Dufferin*.

1881      The *Atatlanta* from Canada loses 2–0 to the *Mischief.*

1885      The centerboard cutter *Puritan* wins over England's *Genesta* 2–0.

1886      The *Mayflower,* another Burgess design for the New York Yacht Club, bests England's *Galaten*, 2–0.

1887      The Burgess-designed, Pusey & Jones–built *Volunteer* scuttles Scotland's *Thistle*, 2–0.

1893    Herreshoff creates a truly great design in the *Vigilant* and wins 3–0 against the *Valkyrie II*.

1895    Herreshoff's *Defender* sinks the *Valkyrie III* in three straight races.

1899    Sir Thomas Lipton's *Shamrock* loses to Herreshoff's *Columbia* 3–0.

1901    Herreshoff's *Columbia* wins again, 3–0, over the *Shamrock II*.

1903    Sixteen thousand square feet of sail on the Herreshoff-designed *Reliance* triumphs over Lipton's *Shamrock III*.

1920    The First World War and other events leave a gap in Cup races until Lipton challenges with the *Shamrock IV* to win two but lose three straight against Herreshoff's last Cup boat, the *Resolute*.

1930    The boats of the J-class series debut at over 80 feet in length, with masts as tall as 165 feet. Vanderbilt's *Enterprise* meets Lipton's *Shamrock V* in Rhode Island Sound, winning 4–0.

1934    The defender *Rainbow* beats T.O.M. Sopwith's challenger, the *Endeavour*, 3–2.

1937    The New York Yacht Club's "Super J," the *Ranger*, beats the *Endeavour II* in four straight.

1958    The New York Yacht Club's *Columbia* whips England's *Sceptre*, 4–0.

1962    Australia challenges with Alan Payne's *Gretel* losing to the New York Yacht Club yacht W*eatherly*, 4–1.

1964    The *Constellation* swamps England's *Sovereign*, 4–0.

1967    Australia's *Dame Pattie* loses to Sparkman and Stephen's *Intrepid* 4–0.

1970      The introduction of the multiple-challenger concept. The *Gretel II* defeats the *France I* and Sweden's *Sverige* to challenge the *Intrepid*. The *Intrepid* easily wins the defender selection trials against the *American Eagle*, the *Heritage* and the *Valiant* to defend the Cup. The *Intrepid* successfully defends the Cup with a 4–1 win.

1974      Dennis Conner as helmsman on the *Courageous* beats the *Intrepid* to defend. The *Courageous* goes on to defeat Alan Bond's Australian boat, *Southern Cross*, 4–0.

1977      Ted Turner's *Courageous* whips the *Australia*, 4–0, which had defeated the *Gretel II*, the *France I* and Sweden's *Sverige* to become the challenger.

1980      The *Freedom* with Dennis Conner defeats Ted Turner and Russell Long and then has a historic win over Bond's *Australia*, 4–1.

1983      The stage is set; the so-called winged keel helps Australia wrest the Cup from the New York Yacht Club after 132 years as the *Australia II* wins, 4–3, over the *Liberty*. The Cup leaves America and goes to Perth, Australia.

1987      A true world match: thirteen challengers, six from the United States. The *Stars & Stripes* from the San Diego Yacht Club, with a Conner-Burnham team, slams Australia's defender, the *Kookaburra III*, in four straight.

1988      A lopsided match between a giant *New Zealand* maxi boat against Dennis Conner's double-hulled catamaran, the *Stars & Stripes*. The San Diego Yacht Club's *Stars & Stripes* wins, 2–0.

1992      Bill Koch aboard his Bristol, Rhode Island Custom Sailboats–built *America³* successfully defends the Cup against Italy's *Il Moro di Venezia*.

1995      Peter Blake and his *Black Magic* out sail *Stars & Stripes* (ex–*Young America*), returning the Cup to New Zealand.

2000      New Zealand, with the *Black Magic*, keeps the Cup by sweeping Italy's *Luna Rossa*.

2003      World-class sailing by Switzerland's *Alinghi* takes the Cup away from the *Black Magic*.

2007      The *Alinghi* whips Emirates team, the *New Zealand*, 5–2.

2010      The Golden Gate Yacht Club trimaran *BMW Oracle* takes the Cup, 2–0, over Société Nautique de Geneve catamaran *Alinghi*.

# NOTES

## CHAPTER 3

1. Paine was born in Boston, Massachusetts, on August 26, 1834. He died at age eighty-two on August 12, 1916. He made his fortune in railroad investments. In his later life, Paine took a great interest in yachting. He was the owner of the *Puritan*, the *Mayflower* and the *Volunteer*, each of which successfully defended the America's Cup against British challengers.

## CHAPTER 4

2. Windham Thomas Wyndham-Quin, fourth Earl of Dunraven.
3. New York Yacht Club member Ogden Goelet donated two historically important yacht race cups—the Goelet Cup for schooners, valued at $1,000, and the Goelet Cup for sloops, valued at $500—for races held in Newport. These cups remained in continual annual competition until Goelet's death in 1899.

# CHAPTER 5

4. Iselin profile courtesy of the Herreshoff Marine Museum.
5. Stephen's profile courtesy of the Herreshoff Marine Museum.
6. Dennis Conner and Michael Levitt, *The America's Cup: The History of Sailing's Greatest Competition in the Twentieth Century* (New York: St. Martin's Press, 1985).

# CHAPTER 6

7. Used with permission of the Herreshoff Museum & America's Cup Hall of Fame, Bristol, Rhode Island, www.herreshoff.org.

# CHAPTER 8

8. For more on the J-boats, see my books *The Herreshoff Yachts* (Charleston, SC: The History Press, 2007) and *America's Cup Trials & Triumphs* (Charleston, SC: The History Press, 2010).

# CHAPTER 11

9. In 1981, the Robert E. Derecktor Shipyard occupied former U.S. Navy piers at Coddington Cove, Newport, building U.S. Coast Guard cutters.

# CHAPTER 14

10. The name *Kanza* comes from the Native American tribe that gave Koch's home state, Kansas, its name. The Kanza people, now the Kaw Indians, are known as the "wind people"; ergo, the boat *Kanza* was designed for wind over ten knots.

# CHAPTER 15

11. The Twenty-ninth America's Cup was contested by the winner of the 1995 Citizen Cup, team Dennis Conner, with the yacht *Stars & Stripes* (ex–*Young America*, USA 36), and the winner of the 1995 Louis Vuitton Cup, team New Zealand, with the yacht *Black Magic* (NZL 32).

# BIBLIOGRAPHY

The text, photographs and illustrations for *The Quest for America's Cup Sailing to Victory* are from diverse sources, and every effort was made to identify those sources. Generally, text is derived from vintage and contemporary newspapers, books, sports magazines and yacht syndicate promotional pamphlets. The authors of long sequences of directly quoted text are identified when known; usually, this text is in the public domain. In addition, selected pages of *Yachting*, *Scientific-American*, *Time*, *Sailing World* and *Sports Illustrated* were consulted in the preparation of this book. All black-and-white illustrations are from the author's collection, and all color photographs are courtesy of Onne van der Wal Photography.

Bavier, Bob. *America's Cup Fever*. New York: Ziff-Davis Pub. Co., 1980.

BMW Oracle Racing Syndicate promotional publication, 2007.

Conner, Dennis, and Michael Levitt. *The America's Cup: The History of Sailing's Greatest Competition in the Twentieth Century*. New York: St. Martin's Press, 1998.

Hammond, Geoffrey F. *Showdown in Newport*. New York: Walden Publications, 1974.

Herreshoff, Francis L. *An Introduction to Yachting*. New York: Sheridan House, 1963.

Herreshoff, Nathanael G. *Recollections*. Edited by Carlton J. Pinheiro. N.p.: Herreshoff Marine Museum, 1998.

# BIBLIOGRAPHY

Hoyt, Edwin P. *The Defenders*. New York: A.S. Barnes and Co., 1969.

Jones, Ted. *Newport and the America's Cup Challenge '77*. New York: W.W. Norton & Co., Inc., 1978.

Parkinson, John, Jr. *History of the New York Yacht Club*. N.p., 1975.

*Providence Journal Bulletin*, selected news items, 1980–95.

Royal Perth Yacht Club. *Official Programme*. 1987.

Swedish Challenge Syndicate promotional publication. 1980.

# INDEX

**A**

*Alinghi* 41, 94, 96, 115
*Alinghi5* 115
*America* 11, 13–15, 18, 20,
    21, 32, 52, 76, 90,
    121, 122
*America³* 43, 83, 85, 91,
    92, 95, 105, 107,
    108, 111
*American Eagle* 39
*Australia* 39, 98
*Australia II* 40, 41, 42, 83,
    85, 102

**B**

Bertrand, John 42, 102, 108
*Black Magic* 87, 112, 115
*BMW Oracle* 41, 115
Bond, Alan 39, 40, 41,
    42, 102
Burgess, Edward 14, 23,
    24, 25, 26, 72, 77
Burgess, Starling 24, 37, 76

**C**

*Challenge Australia* 110
Civil War 12, 14, 24

*Colonia* 26
*Columbia* 16, 20, 33, 35,
    38, 47, 48, 53, 67
Conner, Dennis 38, 39,
    40, 42, 43, 85, 88,
    90, 92, 101, 112,
    122
*Constellation* 38, 87
*Courageous* 36, 38, 39, 97, 99

**D**

*Dame Pattie* 39
*Dauntless* 21
Deed of Gift 33, 41, 72, 87
*Defender* 16, 20, 28, 29, 30,
    33, 34
*Defiance* 55, 56
*Defiant* 43, 92, 105, 107
*Dorade* 37
Dunraven 26, 29, 31, 33,
    34, 45, 121

**E**

Eastern Yacht Club 15, 24
*Endeavour* 35, 38, 78, 79
*Endeavour II* 35, 79
*Enterprise* 60, 71, 72, 99

**F**

*Fanny* 21
Fay, Michael 41
Ficker, Bill 37
Forbes, Robert Bennet 11
*France* 39
*Freedom* 38, 39, 90, 99, 101

**G**

*Genesta* 23, 24
Gerrard, Silversmiths
    Ltd. 9
*Gloriana* 26
Goelet Cup 28
Goetz, Eric 43, 83, 88,
    90, 91, 95
Golden Gate Yacht Club 115
*Gracie* 21
*Gretel* 39, 42, 98
*Gretel II* 39, 42, 98

**H**

Hall, Eric 93
Hardy, Sir James Gilbert 39
Herreshoff, Captain Nat 16,
    26, 29, 37, 47, 52,
    54, 65, 81, 83, 122

Herreshoff, L. Francis 56, 57, 74
Herreshoff Manufacturing Company 30, 34, 38, 49, 55, 72, 76, 81, 93
Herreshoff Marine Museum 43
Hood, Ted 36

**I**

IACC Rule 70
*Il Moro di Venezia* 43, 87, 105, 110
*Independence* 99
International Rule 67, 71
*Intrepid* 36, 37, 38, 87, 99
Iselin, C. Oliver 33

**J**

*Jayhawk* 43, 105, 107
J-boats 71
*Jubilee* 26

**K**

*Kanza* 109
Koch, William Ingraham 42
*Kookaburra III* 40

**L**

*Liberty* 103
*Lionheart* 98
Lipton, Sir Thomas Johnstone 35, 45
Louis Vuitton Cup 98, 105, 110, 111

**M**

*Maria* 18, 23
*Mariner* 36, 39
*Mayflower* 24, 121
Meyer, Elizabeth 75, 79
*Mighty Mary* 43, 85, 92, 114
*Mischief* 21, 24

**N**

New York Yacht Club 11, 12, 13, 20, 24, 29, 31, 32, 33, 34, 39, 41, 52, 54, 55, 60, 67, 68, 69, 71, 102, 103, 121
*New Zealand* 41, 94, 110, 122
Nicholson, Charles E. 55
*Nippon* 110

**O**

*One-Australia* 87

**P**

Paine, Charles J. 24, 25, 75
Paine, John B. 26
*Pilgrim* 26, 28
*Puritan* 23, 24, 121

**R**

*Rainbow* 72, 75, 76, 77
*Ranger* 37, 77
*Reliance* 35, 49, 51, 65
*Resolute* 55, 56, 57, 58, 81
Royal New Zealand Yacht Squadron 9
Royal Perth Yacht Club 42, 102, 103
Royal Ulster Yacht Club 35
Royal Yacht Squadron 9, 11, 13, 26, 35

**S**

San Diego Yacht Club 40, 43, 105, 111, 112
*Sappho* 21
*Shamrock* 35, 42, 45, 55, 57
*Shamrock II* 47
*Shamrock III* 49, 56
*Shamrock IV* 54, 57, 81
*Shamrock V* 60, 71, 74
Sopwith, T.O.M. 35, 72, 75, 78, 79

*Southern Cross* 39, 42, 98
Sparkman & Stephens 38, 92
*Stars & Stripes* 41, 43, 86, 88, 92, 105, 112, 122
Stephens, Olin 36, 37, 38, 77, 87, 99, 101
Stevens, John C. 11, 13, 14, 18, 32, 77, 122
Stevens, Robert Livingston 18
Stewart and Binney 26
*Sverige* 39, 97

**T**

*Thistle* 25
Turner, Robert E. (Ted), III 38, 99
*Tutukaka* 87
Twelve-Meter Rule 69

**U**

Universal Rule 65

**V**

*Valiant* 42, 119
*Valkyrie II* 26, 28
*Valkyrie III* 29, 31, 50
*Vanitie* 56, 81
*Velsheda* 81
*Vigilant* 16, 26, 28, 31, 33, 34
*Vim* 38
*Volunteer* 25, 34, 38, 121

**W**

*Weetamoe* 76
*Whirlwind* 74

**Y**

*Yankee* 23, 24, 75
*Young America* 112

# ABOUT THE AUTHOR

Richard V. Simpson is a native Rhode Islander who has always lived within walking distance of Narragansett Bay, first in the Edgewood section of Cranston and then in Bristol, where he has lived since 1960.

A graphic designer by trade, he worked in advertising, printing, display and textile design studios. He designed and built parade floats for Kaiser Aluminum's Bristol plant and the navy in Newport, Rhode Island.

Richard Simpson displays his proposed poster for the 1976 Bristol celebration of the American Revolution Bicentennial. *Photo by Bob LaChance.*

After retiring in 1996 from a twenty-nine-year federal civil service career with the U.S. Navy Supply Center and Naval Undersea Warfare Center, he began a second career as an author of books on subjects of historical interest in Rhode Island's East Bay with his principal focus on Bristol. This is Richard's seventeenth published title and his fourth with the America's Cup as its subject.

Richard and his wife, Irene, are antique dealers doing business as Bristol Art Exchange; they received their Rhode Island retail sales license in 1970.

Beginning in 1985, he acted as a contributing editor for the national monthly *Antiques & Collecting Magazine*, in which eighty-five of his articles have appeared.

Bristol's famous Independence Day celebration and parade was the subject of Richard's first venture in writing a major history narrative. His 1989 *Independence Day: How the Day Is Celebrated in Bristol, Rhode Island* is the singular authoritative book on the subject; his many anecdotal Fourth of July articles have appeared in the local *Bristol Phoenix* and the *Providence Journal*. His history of Bristol's Independence Day celebration is the source of a story in the July 1989 *Yankee Magazine* and July 4, 2010 issue of *Parade Magazine*.

# BOOKS BY RICHARD V. SIMPSON

*A History of the Italian-Roman Catholic Church in Bristol, RI* (1967)
*Independence Day: How the Day Is Celebrated in Bristol, RI* (1989)
*Old St. Mary's: Mother Church in Bristol, RI* (1994)
*Bristol, Rhode Island: In the Mount Hope Lands of King Philip* (1996)
*Portsmouth, Rhode Island, Pocasset: Ancestral Lands of the Narragansett* (1997)
*Tiverton and Little Compton, Rhode Island: Pocasset and Sakonnet* (1997)
*Tiverton and Little Compton, Rhode Island: Volume II* (1998)
*Bristol, Rhode Island: The Bristol Renaissance* (1998)
*America's Cup Yachts: The Rhode Island Connection* (1999)
*Building the Mosquito Fleet: U.S. Navy's First Torpedo Boats* (2001)
*Bristol: Montaup to Poppasquash* (2002)
*Bristol, Rhode Island: A Postcard History* (2005)
*Narragansett Bay: A Postcard History* (2005)
*Herreshoff Yachts: Seven Generations of Industrialists, Inventors and Ingenuity in Bristol* (2007)
*Historic Bristol: Tales from an Old Rhode Island Seaport* (2008)
*The America's Cup: Trials and Triumphs* (2010)